DATE DUE

3 Jul'63 PK

24 Jul'63 FA

14 Aug 6 3 MP

24 Sep/63 FA

NOV 0 3 1989
NOV 3 0 1985

NOV 0 2 1989 RET

DEC 22 1989 RET

DEC 22 1989 RET

Nationalism in Latin America

OTHER BOOKS BY ARTHUR P. WHITAKER

The Spanish American Frontier

The Mississippi Question

*The United States and
the Independence of Latin America*

The Huancavelica Mercury Mines

*The United States and
South America: The Northern Republics*

The Western Hemisphere Idea

The United States and Argentina

*Argentine Upheaval: Perón's Fall and
the New Regime*

Spain and Defense of the West

EDITOR

*Documents Concerning Spanish
Commercial Policy in the Floridas*

Latin America and the Enlightenment

Inter-American Affairs: An Annual Survey

University of Florida Press
Gainesville - 1962

PAST
AND
PRESENT

ARGENTINA
BOLIVIA
BRAZIL
CHILE
COLOMBIA
COSTA RICA
CUBA
DOMINICAN REPUBLIC
ECUADOR
GUATEMALA
HAITI
HONDURAS
MEXICO
NICARAGUA
PANAMA
PARAGUAY
PERU
EL SALVADOR
URUGUAY
VENEZUELA

Nationalism in Latin America

ARTHUR P. WHITAKER

To Alix

A University of Florida Press Book

COPYRIGHT, 1962, BY THE BOARD OF COMMISSIONERS
OF STATE INSTITUTIONS OF FLORIDA

ALL RIGHTS RESERVED

LIBRARY OF CONGRESS CATALOGUE CARD NO. 62-17696

PRINTED BY THE MILLER PRESS, JACKSONVILLE, FLORIDA

By Way
of
Introduction

Each year our Department of History sponsors a series of lectures on American civilization delivered by one of the leading Americanists of our day. In previous years the lectures were given by Professors John Allen Krout, Holman Hamilton, Perry Miller, and John D. Hicks. It is indeed a genuine pleasure to welcome Dr. Arthur P. Whitaker to this distinguished company.

Dr. Whitaker, Latin Americanist and professor of history at the University of Pennsylvania, speaks with authority on nationalism in Latin America. These essays are timely and appropriate. Nationalism, an English and western European invention, has been one of Europe's most universally accepted exports. Some form of it has been adopted by even the newest nations with peoples still in a tribal stage of social organization.

Even though its strength is waning in Europe, nationalism's importance is growing in all the so-called

NATL'm
AS A Political
Force.

underdeveloped countries. Americans must understand
Latin America's particular experience with nationalism,
for our knowledge of the forces which inspire our hemi-
spheric neighbors should be thorough.

Professor Whitaker points out that Latin American
nationalism early demonstrated certain characteristics
such as its "continentalism" and its "positive and humane" aspects. He follows it through its various transformations, notably the addition of strong economic,
cultural, military, and political elements. He concludes
his global, local, and continental perspectives of Latin
American nationalism with the comment that, despite the
problems it raises, it is "an asset to the United States and
the free world at large, for it is the most effective of all
barriers against penetration of the area by the Sino-Soviet
bloc." We are deeply grateful to Professor Whitaker for
his cogent and penetrating analysis of this complex but
vital force.

conclusion .
good pt.

J. WAYNE REITZ, *President*
University of Florida

The Author's
Personal
Acknowledgments

L ate in March, 1961, it was my privilege to give the
American Civilization Lectures at the University of
Florida. My subject was nationalism in Latin America
and there were three lectures. Somewhat expanded and
revised for publication, but otherwise substantially in their
original form, they are now presented in print, thanks
again to the generosity of the gentlemen of Gainesville.

These three essays, as the lectures have now become,
do not pretend to be anything more than a preliminary
reconnaissance of a large and complex problem. Even so,
my venture may well seem foolhardy, if only because the
Latin American countries are so numerous and diverse
and because, as the title of this little volume suggests, I
have undertaken to deal both with their tenebrous past
and their tumultuous present. In extenuation I can only
say that this important subject deserves far more system-
atic study than it has yet received and that I hope such
study may be stimulated by the present reconnaissance,

if only by way of negative reaction. I, for one, plan to continue the exploration.

Since 1959 my interest in this subject has had its main focus in the study of Argentine nationalism carried on at the University of Pennsylvania under my direction. My thanks are due to the Rockefeller Foundation for its considerable aid to that program, out of which the present volume grew. They are also due to the following graduate students participating in the program, whose investigations of particular aspects of Argentine nationalism, past and present, have been useful to me: Earl Glauert, on Ricardo Rojas as an exponent of nationalism; Marvin Goldwert, on the changing role of the Argentine army; James R. Levy, on José de San Martín as a symbol of nationalism; and Winthrop R. Wright, on railways and economic nationalism.

I am indebted to William Ebenstein of Princeton University and to Ricardo Caillet-Bois, Director of the Instituto de Historia Argentina "Dr. Emilio Ravignani," of Buenos Aires, for reading the original manuscript, and to Hans Kohn, outstanding authority on the history of nationalism, for reading the revised manuscript. Though they did not read my manuscript, Professors José Luis Romero and Gino Germani of the University of Buenos Aires were most helpful where Argentina was concerned.

For their hospitality when my wife and I visited the University of Florida on the occasion of these lectures, we are grateful to many persons there. Special acknowledgments go to Donald E. Worcester, who, when chairman of the History Department several years ago, invited me to give these lectures, and to Lyle N. McAlister, who, as chairman at the time of our visit, was our official and ever thoughful host, and who has since had the task of coping with the completed work.

Table
of
Contents

From Europe
to Latin
America

1. In Latin America nationalism is as old as national independence, which began a century and a half ago, and its form and content have varied materially from time to time and from country to country in that highly diversified area. Yet, whatever modifications the local environment may have brought about in them, the manifold expressions of Latin American nationalism are no exception to the rule that, in the world at large, modern nationalism has its roots in Western Europe. The European background is particularly apposite to the case of Latin America, for modern nationalism took shape in Europe during the era of the French Revolution and Napoleon, and it was just at the close of this era that the new states of Latin America began their struggle for independence. Moreover, both then and subsequently, the leaders of the new states were profoundly influenced by the evolving concept of nationalism as manifested both

in its European homeland and in Europe's graft on North America, the United States.

The present chapter will accordingly begin with an account of the meaning of modern nationalism and its manifestations in Europe and the United States since the late eighteenth century. It will then, against this background, sketch the checkered history of nationalism in Latin America. As regards all three areas, stress will be laid on the functional aspect of nationalism. As regards Latin America, it will also be laid on the fact that, while the Latin Americans have always borrowed freely from abroad, they have been no less free in adapting these borrowings to their special circumstances and needs. As a result, in recent decades the widening gap between their economic, social, and political development and that of Western Europe and the United States has been reflected in a divergence of their variety of nationalism from its European prototype and the North American model. Most recently it has also been reflected in the assimilation of the Latin American type in some respects to the nationalism of the new states of Asia and Africa.

2. In the present state of the discussion of nationalism, it seems advisable to preface any effort to determine its meaning with two caveats, one against confusing the issue by a misuse of value judgments, the other against the current tendency to identify the term exclusively with its aggressive or xenophobic manifestations.

Where any broad sweep of history is involved, as it is here, the protean term "nationalism" has always eluded generally acceptable definition. Description, on the other hand, is relatively easy, but even this is too often flawed by the injection of value judgments based on incomplete evidence. To many recent writers of the liberal persuasion, for example, nationalism has become a dirty word signifying at best a pathological variant of patriotism and at worst a reactionary brand of authoritarianism. Thus, a leading Swiss historian, Herbert Lüthy, describes nationalism as "a terrorist theory which imposes conformity in ideas and conduct."[1] That fits some situations but distorts others. Among the latter is the one generally prevailing in Western Europe in the first half of the nineteenth century, when nationalism was espoused by liberals and opposed by that pillar of absolutism, Prince Metternich. Nationalism in any general sense is a spirit, not a program; a tool or instrument, not a purpose. As Ernest Barker said in this connection, "We can only judge tools by the efficiency with which they fulfil the purposes for which they are used; and if we pass any moral judgment, it can only be passed on purposes."[2]

The purposes served by nationalism have been many and diverse, but, from the point of view of the nation concerned, all of them fall into one or the other of two categories: those that are directed inward, towards the nation's domestic concerns; and those that are directed outward, towards its relations with other nations or peoples. Because the world has suffered so much from aggressive nationalism in the past hundred years, the latter category is the one that comes most readily to mind. For this very reason, however, we must take special pains to preserve a proper balance by pointing out that the first category, too, is a numerous one. It comprises not only most of the nationalist movements of early nineteenth-century Europe, but also many later ones and a large proportion of the expressions of nationalism of all periods in England, the United States, and, until recently, Latin America. In these cases, the primary intent of nationalism was, not aggrandizement at the expense of outsiders, *primary focus of Nat'lism in L.A.

but preservation and promotion of internal unity in the face of domestic particularisms of one kind or another.

But just what do we mean by nationalism? According to Hans Kohn, one of its keenest exegetes, nationalism is "first and foremost a state of mind, an act of consciousness"—specifically, "the individual's identification of himself with the 'we-group' to which he gives supreme loyalty." "In different periods of history, and in different civilizations," continues Kohn, "we find different groups to which this supreme loyalty is given"; since the French Revolution it has been given increasingly to the nation. Yet while "nationalism as a group-consciousness is . . . a psychological and social fact," it cannot be explained in psychological or sociological terms alone, for nationality is a historical and a political concept. Moreover, nationalities are the ever changing products of the living forces of history; they "come into existence only when certain objective bonds delimit a social group," but while a nationality generally has several of these attributes—common descent, language, territory, political entity, customs and traditions, and religion—"very few have all of them."[3]

Carlton Hayes, another leading authority, defines nationalism as "a fusion of patriotism with a consciousness of nationality" and nationality as a product of cultural and historical forces—specifically, a product combining "a common language (or closely related dialects) and . . . a community of historical traditions." Hayes, too, stresses "the fluidity of nationalities in the long run of history." He differentiates sharply between cultural nationalism and political nationalism, holding that when the cultural bases of nationality become "by some process of education . . . the object of popular emotional patriotism, the result is nationalism." His latest work deals with the important theme of nationalism as religion and maintains that nationalism usually becomes "a paramount, a supreme loyalty" only when it is "fused with religious emotion" and "becomes a religion or a substitute for religion."[4]

Recognizing the need for greater precision in the study of nationalism, historians have begun to look to the other social sciences for help, and some has been forthcoming. Perhaps the most direct and greatest aid has been given by anthropologists, in two ways: first, in exposing the fallacy of racial ideas that once clouded the whole question; and second, in renewing with fresh method the attack on the ancient and highly controverted problem of national character. Sociologists, including some in Latin America, have aided with studies of the attitudes of social groups, the assimilation of immigrants, and in other ways.[5] Much is expected of social psychology and depth psychology as they develop.[6] Precisely because political scientists resemble historians so closely in their approach to nationalism, less is expected of them.

The most thorough and comprehensive application of social science methods that has been made to this problem is the work of a man who at the time was a professor of history, Karl W. Deutsch.[7] Dissatisfied with the results achieved by the empirical and intuitive methods employed in all previous studies of the subject, Deutsch attacked the problem with the aid of communications theory and cybernetics. The result was a functional definition of "nationality," a term which he preferred to "nationalism." Instead of the conventional cultural, political, and economic factors (one or more of which he found often missing in any given situation), he proposed that the test of nationality be made the ability of the members of a group to communicate more effectively and more broadly with their fellow members than with nonmembers.

Among students of nationalism Deutsch's approach is most attractive to those seeking for means of quantitative measurement and prediction, but all students are indebted to him for stressing the significance of certain aspects of the problem, such as social assimilation and mobilization. At the same time, the validity of his approach is limited in a number of ways. It requires data that are often meager or nonexistent; this is true of all of Latin America in the nineteenth century and of most of it in the twentieth century. Also, even when the data are abundant, no statistical study is better than its basic assumptions, and Deutsch's method gives no assurance that these will be sound. Yet again, it concentrates on the questions how and to what extent national sentiment spreads; it throws little light on other questions of great interest to historians, such as what nationalism is and why it rises and spreads. Finally, its scope is unduly limited by the apparent assumption that true nationalism can be said to exist only when supported by a national consensus. Here, on the other hand, it is assumed that nationalism is analogous to religion, and as varied in its expressions; that several different types of nationalism may coexist in a given country and that all of them merit study; and that the dominant type may achieve and maintain dominance otherwise than through the support of a national consensus, since issues are complex and in any society, even the most democratic, large numbers of people are political ciphers.

In short, while quantification can be most useful in dealing with certain aspects of the history of nationalism, particularly in the present statistical century, the conventionally empirical and intuitive methods of the historian are still indispensable for the study of the subject, including its latest phase. The alternative is for the historian to await with folded arms the design, production, and delivery of tools that may possibly never arrive, or which, when they arrive, may prove unsuited to the materials he has to work with.

3. Accordingly, with a frank admission of my reliance on empirical and intuitive tools, as well as on the abundant materials produced with their aid by my predecessors, I suggest the more extended use of functional interpretation in the study of the history of nationalism. I say "more extended use," for previous writers have already employed it extensively in a great variety of situations. What I am suggesting is simply that it be applied to all situations. It is quite different from Deutsch's functional definition of nationalism, for it is not a definition at all. It is only a description of the manifold functions that the complex idea of nationalism has performed in the hands of the highly assorted groups—liberal and reactionary, republican and monarchical, democratic and authoritarian, clerical and anticlerical, upper-class, middle-class, and proletarian—at various times and places since Western Europe and the United States made nationalism one of the dominant ideas of the modern age. Uses of this approach will be illustrated in the following brief sketch of the main stages of the development of modern nationalism.[8] It begins with Western Europe and fans out from there to the United States and other parts of the world, including Latin America.

Although nationalism began its world-wide spread in the era of the French Revolution, there were important anticipations. The most important of these was provided by seventeenth-century England. Even earlier, Renaissance writers in Italy, Germany, and France had been "inspired to a new feeling of patriotism . . . by their

—Whitaker.

identification with classical authors," but "this Renaissance nationalism remained confined to [a] small educated class . . . and was therefore only a passing phenomenon, quickly to be engulfed by the rising tide of the new theologizing" of the Reformation.[9]

The case of England was quite different. From the time of the Tudors to the Puritan Revolution, a then unique concatenation of four prime factors in the nationalist process—linguistic, political, economic, and religious—had by the mid-seventeenth-century produced the first example of modern nationalism. Like the classic type of nationalism cast by the French Revolution a hundred and fifty years later, this English nationalism "became a bond uniting the whole people." But it differed from the French in two ways: it was not secularized, and it was relatively benign. One of its essential ingredients was religion. That this changed through various shadings of Anglicanism and Puritanism makes no difference, for it was always England's own religion. Another such ingredient was the new conception of natural law and reason, which was fundamentally liberal and which produced in England a nationalism of the kind that "runs easily and naturally into internationalism."[10]

From the point of view of the present study, this seventeenth-century English nationalism is of special interest for two reasons. First, it developed at a time when England was sore beset, so that, far from being aggressive, its primary function was to promote national defense. All but specialists tend to exaggerate the isolation and the security of England during this formative period as a result of her insularity. They forget that the seas are not a wall but a highway, and that the seas around England are a defensive moat only when she can defend them with superior sea power. In the sixteenth and seventeenth centuries England, not yet mistress of the seas, was constantly exposed to attack by a succession of formidable maritime rivals—first Spain, then the Dutch, and finally France. In the second place, England's seventeenth-century nationalism was transmitted to her North American colonies, where it provided the basis for the first phase of nationalism in the United States.[11] The latter in turn helped to shape the nationalism of the new states of Latin America.

A new source, the Enlightenment, had been added by the time the United States began to develop a nationalism of its own under the general impulse of a growing sense of separateness called Americanism and under the special pressure of the conflict with the metropolis after 1763. The Enlightenment, however, served largely to reinforce the liberal and benign character of the nationalism inherited from England. Also, like the English, the American variety was primarily defensive, and for two generations circumstances combined to keep it so, for until the 1820's the United States, a relatively weak power, felt itself encircled and threatened by European powers rooted in America—Great Britain, Spain, and France.

Nevertheless, still other circumstances impressed three distinctive features on American nationalism. One was the integrative function that it performed in filling the void created by the destruction of British authority over the thirteen colonies. As has often been noted, down to the eve of the American Revolution the colonies had more trouble with one another than with Britain and it was the latter that maintained a modicum of union and harmony among them. When the British tie was severed, a replacement had to be found in order to prevent disintegration and chaos, and this was provided by a nascent nationalism which, however slow to develop and however variously defined by Hamiltonians and Jeffersonians and their successors, was still nationalism. A similar role soon began to be played by nationalism in filling voids created in Europe by the French Revolution and in Latin America by the independence movement of 1810-1825, but the case of the United States was the first of this kind.

Another distinctive feature involved the United States' relations with the new states of Latin America. It resulted from the early nineteenth-century fusion of the benign nationalism inherited from England with the mystique of the Western Hemisphere idea—the idea that the peoples of the New World form a coherent, kindred group set apart by Nature and their nature from the wicked, warring peoples of the Old World.[12] From the beginning of its independence, the United States had thought of itself as a regular member of the general family of nations,[13] but this concept was now modified by the newer one of a special relationship with the Latin Americans as fellow members of a subfamily of New World nations. On the other hand, one important feature of the older concept—belief in the equality of all nation-states—remained unchanged for many years. This was the kind of nationalism that the United States communicated to its newly independent neighbors to the south when their own was taking shape and when the foundations of inter-American relations were being laid. Not until the close of the century, when a different type of nationalism was growing up in the United States, did the latter exchange the concept of a coordinate New World family for that of its own hegemony in the Western Hemisphere.

Finally, the United States was the first country to complete the secularization of nationalism, as reflected in the stipulation of its Constitution of 1787 that "Congress shall make no law respecting the establishment of religion." England was moving in the same direction, but had not reached the goal at this time. It still showed vestiges of the Elizabethan doctrine that identified citizenship with churchmanship—that is, with membership in the Church of England; indeed, one of the chief vestiges continued to exist until the passage of the Catholic Emancipation Act in 1829. France, too, moved in the same direction, and did so more quickly and wholeheartedly than England, but it began to move only after the outbreak of its revolution in 1789. The priority of the United States in the development of secular nationalism is clear. In this respect, too, its influence was felt in the new Latin American states, though with less effect than most of its leaders could have wished.

4. After the French Revolution and its self-proclaimed heir, Napoleon, domesticated nationalism on the continent of Europe, the new version started on its worldwide dissemination. It spread first to the new states of Latin America while Napoleon was still in power, but was modified there by the prototype developed in England and the United States. Its diffusion and modification have continued uninterruptedly ever since. Today, nationalism in one form or another is an almost universal phenomenon.

Obviously the history of so vast and complex a process cannot be analyzed here. We can only sketch some of the salient features of the principal stages, and even this sketch must be confined largely to points that are useful for comparison with the case of Latin America. An important aid for such a comparison—and, indeed, for any comparative study of nationalism—has been provided by Hans Kohn in his analysis of the two basic types of nationalism, that of the Western World and that of Central and Eastern Europe and Asia.[14] Of the many illuminating contrasts drawn by Kohn, none is more suggestive or useful—at least in the present state of the world —than the one between the respective forms of society associated with these two types of nationalism: in the Western World, a pluralistic and open society; in Central and Eastern Europe and Asia, an authoritarian and closed society. This antinomy, based on historical generalization, is all the more valuable for the very reason that, as will appear below, quite recent events have tended to blur the distinction somewhat.

Following Carlton Hayes's periodization, which for the nineteenth century is based mainly on developments in Europe, we may regard the first stage of the history of modern nationalism as running from the French Revolution to the 1860's. In the early part of this period the primary function of nationalism was to replace old ties of union destroyed by the age of revolution. Formerly these ties had been provided by absolute monarchies based on the principle of legitimacy, which had given a semblance of national unity to aggregations of disparate communities in which there was still a strong remnant of medieval particularism. As revolution broke the bonds of absolutism and legitimacy, a new cement was needed to hold the body politic together. In accordance with the new principle of popular sovereignty, the need was met by the development of the ideology of nationalism.

At the outset this ideology was an artificial, *ad hoc* construction, not the spontaneous expression of a universal or even a general faith. In some countries of Western Europe, notably Spain, it has not to this day gained general acceptance—the old particularism is still too strong for it.[15] In other countries, however, notably France, where an efficient government promoted it with the whole apparatus of the state, through education, military service, and other means, the ideology of nationalism took firm root and developed an existence of its own, independent of the circumstances that had given rise to it.

Because of the accident of its birth modern nationalism was at first identified with liberalism, and the identification was generally maintained through the first half of the nineteenth century. As everyone knows, liberalism is a relative term, whose meaning depends on the context. In the European context of that period, the meaning was quite clear in its main outlines. It signified in most cases devotion to the principles of popular sovereignty, representative and constitutional government, individual rights of free speech and assembly, and the rule of law. Also, from the start nationalism was equipped with its full panoply of flag, ritual, patriotic hymns, and national heroes.

The new nationalism throve because it was congruous with many elements of the life of Europe at that time. It was mainly the work of the rising middle class, which, unlike the kings and nobles of the old regime, was not cosmopolitan but local-provincial-national in outlook. Economic organization was in the early stage of industrial capitalism and so looked to the nation-state as the best guardian of its welfare. And the optimistic cosmology of the Enlightenment, as filtered down to the nineteenth century by Mazzini and others, promised everyone the achievement of heaven-on-earth through the nation-state.[16]

This was nationalism's liberal phase, when it was constructive at home and cooperative abroad. Its primary function was the domestic one of serving as the integrative ideology of the new popular-sovereignty type of state. In foreign relations it aimed at promoting peace and good will and sharing the benefits of freedom. As already noted, it was during this first phase of European nationalism that the new nations of Latin America emerged and took shape.

The opening of a new phase was heralded, and in large part explained, by the collapse of the liberal revolutions of 1848 in Europe. Nationalism proved stronger than liberalism. When liberal leadership failed to realize national aspirations, the leadership passed to other hands and nationalism took on a new character. To be more accurate, it took on a variety of new characters, for it differed from one country to another and from one period to another in the same country.

In the sense that its divorce from early nineteenth-century liberalism has been permanent, and that it became identified instead with forcefulness or intolerance or imperialism or authoritarianism, or all of these together, this period of nationalism has lasted down to the present. Closer analysis, however, distinguishes three phases: The first, to World War I, was one of both militant nationalism, best represented by the Germany of Bismarck and Wilhelm II, and national imperialism, represented by all the great powers, including Great Britain and the United States as well as France, Germany, Italy, Russia, and Japan. The second phase, from the 1920's to World War II, was marked by the totalitarian nationalism of which Fascist Italy, Nazi Germany, and Falangist Spain were the chief exemplars. The most striking feature of the third phase, since 1945, has been the explosion of an ambiguous popular-authoritarian nationalism among the underdeveloped peoples of Asia, Africa, and Latin America, abetted by the national imperialists of the Soviet Union.

5. The foregoing circumstances explain why historians of the politically liberal school find it difficult to discuss the development of nationalism in the past century with sympathy or even with scientific detachment, for to many of them its history can be summed up as the degradation of a once noble idea. In the past decade, however, there has occurred a curious "rehabilitation of nationalism."[17] Its rehabilitation has been due mainly to two factors: the cold war between East and West, and the rapid disintegration of colonial empires since 1945. In both East and West, nationalism has been redeemed from the deep discredit into which it had fallen and, though for quite different reasons, each side has restored it to good standing in the hope that it will prove a potent weapon against the other. Our side invokes it against the Soviet Union in Tito's Yugoslavia, in Poland, Hungary, and other satellite states, while the Communist bloc has used it to blast us in Fidel Castro's Cuba and elsewhere in Latin America, Africa, and Asia.

It should be repeated, however, that in many respects the nationalism of today is quite different from that of earlier times. It differs to some extent even from the nationalism of the period just before World War II and, of course, much more widely from that of the early nineteenth century. The four principal changes may be summarized as follows.

First, some rather sharp differentiations have grown up as regards attitudes towards nationalism. Many of these differentiations can be expressed in geographical terms, though all of them appear to be correlated either with national differences in economic and political development and military power, or with the cold war, or with a combination of the two. In Western Europe, for example, nationalism has been rehabilitated mainly as a cold-war weapon for use in other areas. In any general sense nationalism now finds its chief expression outside Europe, and above all in Africa, Asia, and Latin America, where it serves as the ideological focus of the revolution of rising aspirations.

In the second place, among the many underdeveloped countries that now constitute the great bulk of its devotees, the cult of nationalism has taken on a strong economic coloration. The change is only one of emphasis, for, fundamentally, nationalism remains a political concept. Nevertheless, the new emphasis has had some practical consequences that differentiate the economic nationalism of today not merely in degree but in kind from the "classic" political nationalism of the nineteenth and early twentieth centuries.

Two illustrations will have to suffice. One of these is the reversal of attitudes towards investments of foreign private capital, which were once eagerly sought by nearly all economically backward countries and are now viewed askance by most of them. As we shall see, in none of them has the attitude towards such investments changed more dramatically than in Latin America. The other illustration comes from the Middle East but could just as well have been drawn from Latin America. One Middle Eastern spokesman has put the matter in a nutshell: "Our fathers," he said, "would have stressed the superiority of European [political] institutions and morale" as a standard for their people to measure up to if they wished to achieve independence, whereas the present generation among these peoples think of this problem first of all in terms of "heavy industry, technology, and the scientific aptitudes that make these possible."[18]

The shift from political to economic nationalism is closely related to the third in our list of major alterations.

This is the spread of the authoritarian, closed-society type of nationalism from Central and Eastern Europe and Asia, with which Hans Kohn associated it in his well-known classification of the basic types of nationalism, to other parts of the world. Today, the distributive factor is (economic) rather than geographical, and the underdeveloped countries everywhere seem to be particularly susceptible to the appeal of this type of nationalism. Leading examples of its spread include Castro's Cuba as well as Nasser's Egypt.

The most obvious explanation of this change is that the impatience of the underdeveloped peoples to achieve a better life has led them to abandon the relatively slow processes of economic and political liberalism for the forced-draft speed-up that is deemed to be feasible only when imposed by an authoritarian state. Historically, authoritarianism is as much at home on the right as on the left, but the recent trend in the underdeveloped countries has been towards its identification with left-wing movements. Nationalistic and revolutionary, these movements aim at duplicating the rapid economic and social transformations of the Soviet Union and Red China by imitating their authoritarian methods.

The fourth and last of the recent changes in the nature of nationalism is the decline, in some quarters, of faith in the adequacy of conventional nationalism to the needs of the modern world, and the corresponding rise of what may be called extended or regional or continental nationalism. Examples include Western European union, the Arab League, Pan Africanism, and, last but not least, Pan Latin Americanism. The discussion of this change will be deferred to the last chapter, where it will be confined to the case of Latin America.

6. As suggested at several points above, nationalism in Latin America has always been both like and unlike the European and other varieties in form, content, and function. It has been highly derivative, with Europe as its chief source; hence the resemblances. But, in this as in most other matters, the Latin Americans have modified and naturalized their borrowings; hence the differences. On the one hand, for example, Latin America has made no basic change in the symbols or the vocabulary of nationalism; whereas, on the other hand, Spain's syncretism of nationalism with the official religion has not been reproduced in any of the eighteen Spanish American states. Similar comparisons and contrasts exist as between Latin America and the areas of Asia and Africa in which nationalism is derivative.

It would be doubly misleading, however, to speak of Latin American nationalism as *sui generis,* for that would be to deny a fact and affirm a fiction—the fact of its close kinship to European nationalism, and the fiction that it has developed uniformly throughout Latin America. The truth is that nationalism in Latin America is no exception to the rule that the peoples of that area form a bewildering combination of diversity with unity. Brazil, for example, lagged behind Mexico and Argentina in the development of nationalist feeling, probably for two main reasons. First, Brazil's struggle for independence began much later, was relatively brief and almost bloodless, and was soon followed by Portuguese recognition. Second and possibly more important, independent Brazil had less need of the cement of nationalism because of the continuity of its governing personnel and institutions from the colonial period—a continuity represented by the fact that it was still a monarchy, the Empire of Brazil, and that its monarch was still a member of the Portuguese royal house of Braganza. In Mexico, on the other hand, the break began at the start of what turned out to be a long and bloody conflict, and the first patriot leader, Miguel Hidalgo y Costilla, fought not only for the independence of "the Mexican nation," as he called it, but also for a social revolution to give expression to the ideals of the new nation.[19] How nationalism in Argentina likewise developed at an early date, though along different lines, will appear in the next chapter.

In contrast to the Europe of that period, nationalism in the first generation of independence was qualified by a kind of continentalism or Pan Latin Americanism. We shall have more to say below about this feeling and its persistence to the present time. Here we need only note that it was given expression not only in political plans of confederation or some other sort of union by Simón Bolívar and his contemporaries, but also in "literary Americanism." As one writer has said, perhaps with some exaggeration, of Spanish America: "There is no doubt that while the struggle for independence was going on and for some time after its fulfillment, the idea of national literature referred to an American literature, rather than to a local Argentine, Chilean, Mexican, or other particular literature."[20]

Finally, as contrasted with the United States, in Latin America nationalism developed in a climate of opinion where government was regarded neither as the natural enemy of its citizens or subjects nor as at best a necessary evil ("eternal vigilance is the price of liberty"; "that government governs best which governs least"). Rather, Latin Americans from the start have been disposed to regard government as, at least potentially, a friend and benefactor, as the political expression of a nation identified with its nationals and existing to serve them. Al-

though this view has never been universally held and although, about the turn of the century, for a variety of reasons, it suffered many defections, it has regained its vogue in the past generation. Hence, if there is such a thing as a typically Latin American attitude towards nationalism, this is it. For example, the Latin Americans seem to have a built-in predilection for statism. Though many were converted to laissez faire for a time and some have remained firm in the faith, this predilection reasserted itself in the twentieth century when the winds of foreign nationalism, to which the Latin Americans have always been responsive, began to blow in that direction.

Subject to the usual caveat with regard to generalizations about Latin America, the principal stages in the development of nationalism in that area may be summarized as follows.

From the beginning of independence to the late nineteenth century, Latin America echoed the liberal nationalism of early nineteenth-century Europe and the United States. This was an essentially political age in Latin America and the quality of its nationalism—political, introspective, and liberal—reflected that fact. From the start, in the countries in which nationalism first became articulate, patriotic hymns were written, national flags adopted, and patriotism taught in schools. Boundary disputes were almost the only important source of international controversy, and defense against invasion from outside Latin America was the only substantial ground for international cooperation. Cultural nationalism hardly existed save for a vague literary Americanism; this was the era when the cultural preponderance of France was established throughout most of Latin America. Likewise, economic nationalism was rudimentary. Whereas foreign soldiers who had aided in the fight for independence were

sent packing as soon as it was won, foreign capital and
business enterprise continued for generations to receive
an unqualifiedly cordial welcome that would be incon-
ceivable today.

An important gloss on this period has been added by
Víctor Alba.[21] According to him, a distinctively Latin
American feature of the nationalism of those years, which
has come to the fore again recently, was its combination
of a "positive and humane" character with a devotion to
the improvement of the lot of the individual citizen, and
a preoccupation with this realistic task rather than, as in
Europe, with the doctrinaire assertion of great principles.
If, instead of questioning this somewhat idyllic picture,
we ask why Latin American performance fell so far short
of the ideal, the most plausible answer lies in two lacks.
One was the lack of a strong middle class to carry out
what was, as Europe's experience at this time suggests, an
essentially middle-class operation. The other was the lack
of a strong economy to provide the sinews for "positive
and humane" action.

Since the late nineteenth century four important
changes have taken place in the character of Latin American nationalism. The first began in the 1890's; the
second about 1910; the third in the 1930's; and the
fourth in the 1950's.

The first change was the injection of an economic
content, partly under socialist influence. For example, in
1896 the founder of the Argentine Socialist party, Juan
Bautista Justo, declared in a public address that Great
Britain had achieved through investments a feat that
would have been impossible for her armed forces—the
conquest of Argentina. "We Argentines," he thundered,
"have been reduced by economic penetration to the status
of a British colony!" Subsequently broadened to include

② Battle-
implement
nationalization
program.

① foreign investment
seized in
Uruguay by 1910.

MAJOR
CRITICISM
OF
Foreign
Intervention
by Nationalists
present

all "imperialists" and the corrupt local oligarchy of *vende-patrias* who have "sold out" to the imperialists, this kind of indictment is now one of the chief weapons in the arsenals of nationalists throughout Latin America, as well as in other underdeveloped countries.

These new ideas first became public policy in Uruguay, beginning in 1904 under President José Batlle y Ordóñez; by 1910 foreign investment there had been brought to a standstill. José Enrique Rodó, another Uruguayan, had earlier given an impulse to cultural nationalism in his masterpiece, *Ariel* (1900), which was to have a wide and lasting influence among Latin American intellectuals.

The second change was one of a broader kind. It was brought to focus by the centennial celebrations of independence which from 1910 on gave a strong impulse to nationalism in several Latin American countries, notably Argentina, Chile, Colombia, Venezuela, and Mexico. In some of these nationalism was now provided with more effective leadership by an emergent middle class. About the same time Latin American governments were becoming for the first time practicing members of the family of nations (for nearly all of them the Hague Peace Conference of 1907 was their first top-flight international conference), and some were decking themselves out in the full panoply of a nation-state, complete with an arms race (notably Argentina, Brazil, and Chile) and a power bloc (the same three joined, on second thought, in the ABC bloc).

Nationalism now began to reach full flower in Latin America. It became cultural and economic as well as political and military, and outward-looking rather than introspective. Two outstanding developments of this phase of Latin American nationalism were the cultural nationalism of Ricardo Rojas's *Argentinidad,* benignly packaged but full of dynamite, and the economic nationalism *cum* social revolution that came charging out of Mexico with no suggestion of benignity. Both possess a broad Latin American significance discussed below.

With the third important change in the character of Latin American nationalism we enter upon the penultimate phase of its development to the present time. As described by Víctor Alba,[22] this change began in the 1930's under Communist influence and consisted in the emergence of a new type of Latin American nationalism which was "negative, chauvinistic, sterile, and isolationist." In the minds of its Communist instigators this new nationalism was a weapon of political-cultural warfare: it was designed to divide Latin America from the United States and the rest of the Western world and to facilitate Communist penetration of Latin America by sowing discord and creating confusion among its people. In furtherance of this purpose the Communist conspirators used Latin American intellectuals as their cat's-paws in propagating divisive ideas. They disparaged everything that tended to unite the Latin Americans with one another as well as with the United States and Europe. To this end they fomented a narrow nationalism by playing up the glories of each national culture in Latin America, with special stress in each case on the indigenous culture (Aztec, Maya, Inca, and so on) on which the present-day culture of that particular nation was assumed to be based.

According to Alba, this strategy was quite successful for two decades, but in the past few years—the fourth and final phase to date—Latin American writers have been waking up and are now returning to the pre-1930 type of nationalism. This type he describes as not only positive and humanist, but also as Pan Latin American.

Perhaps he is too sanguine. In any event his conclusion is based on a three-fold assumption which, though formerly sound, has now lost some of its validity. This is the assumption, first, that Latin American intellectuals come from the middle class; second, that they shape the opinions of this class; and third, that through this class they exercise great influence on public opinion and policy throughout Latin America. The doubts about this assumption relate mainly to its second and third parts—the influence of the intellectuals on Latin America's middle groups, and of these groups on the turbulent sea of social ferment in present-day Latin America. Insofar as these propositions are pertinent to our theme of nationalism, more will be said about both of them.

To sum up what has been said so far: Though modern nationalism had its roots in England, it was rounded out and started on its world mission by the French Revolution, just in time to serve the new states that soon emerged in Latin America. Its subsequent development there has at all times reflected the great diversity of Latin America, but in general it is best understood, as in other areas, in terms of its functioning as an instrument of integration and the realization of desired goals. Since Latin America is in most respects underdeveloped or intermediate on the world scale, the goals of its nationalism today are in many ways similar to those of the new states of Asia and Africa. Yet the Latin American states are no longer new; for nearly a century and a half they have been both independent national states and states familiar with the ideology of nationalism. Accordingly, they form an interesting "grey area" between Europe, where nationalism is declining, and Asia and Africa, where it is burgeoning. A particularly vivid illustration is provided by Argentina, which will now be discussed as a case history.

The
Case of
Argentina

1.   One of the largest and, from every point of view, one of the most important of the twenty Latin American countries, Argentina is an excellent subject for a case study of the history of nationalism in that area. To be sure, Argentina is not typical of the rest of Latin America; but neither is Brazil nor even Mexico, and these three countries combined account for nearly two thirds of the population of Latin America. If we eliminate them, what is there left to typify? More to the point, Argentina is representative of Latin America at large in the sense that it is already well advanced in stages of economic, social, cultural, and political development which most of the other Latin American countries are still striving to reach. Hence by tracing Argentina's experience we can hope to illuminate the whole process of the development of Latin American nationalism, past, present, and future.

Perhaps because Argentina has always had close ties with the outside world—ties first and foremost with

Europe—through the ever powerful Buenos Aires, the historical pattern of Argentine nationalism resembles in its main outlines the general pattern sketched in the preceding chapter, although there were some deviations, which will be noted in due course. In the first phase, which extended from the beginning of independence about 1810 to the turn of the century, Argentine nationalism was essentially introspective, liberal, and benevolent save during the interlude of the Rosas tyranny in the 1830's and '40's; and at all times its chief function was to combat particularism and promote union. The second phase, from the 1890's to the 1940's, was marked increasingly by cultural and economic nationalism and xenophobia, combined with a growing concern for Argentina's international role and, towards the close, an expansionist, aggressive spirit. The third phase, from the 1940's to the present, is more difficult to characterize, partly because it is so recent, but still more because of the fragmentation that Argentine society has suffered in the past generation. But the most distinctive trait of this period seems to be the trend towards harnessing nationalism to a social revolution in the interest of the masses— those called *descamisados* under the Perón regime.

All periodizations are artificial and in some degree misleading. The one just offered is no exception to the rule, but it should at least help the reader to keep his bearings as he makes his way through the more detailed account of the process that follows. This account will in turn, it is hoped, correct any misconceptions by putting flesh on the bare bones of the foregoing outline. It will, among other things, lay due stress throughout on a capitally important theme only alluded to at the end of the outline, namely the relation of social change to the development of nationalism.

2. Thanks to Great Britain, nationalism got off to a flying start in Argentina and began to take shape even before the struggle for independence from Spain began. The reference is, of course, to the British attempts of 1806-1807 to seize Buenos Aires, their repulse by the citizenry with little or no aid from Spain, and the outburst of Argentine pride to which this exploit gave rise. It was celebrated as an *Argentine* triumph—that was precisely the title (*El triunfo argentino*) of a poem by one of the best-known bards of this generation, Vicente López y Planes, that both gave this pride its best literary expression and also helped to bring about, years later, the adoption of "Argentina" as the name of the new nation-state. The name had a double attraction for Argentine nationalists. On the one hand, it was well established in local literary usage going back to the sixteenth century. On the other hand, it was a neologism in official nomenclature, for Spain had never used it to designate any political unit in this area. Hence "Argentina" evoked the past and yet was untainted by association with the Spanish oppressor, and its novelty in the political context strengthened its appeal to the many Argentines who were conscious of their country's mission as one of the first republics of the New World.

Hardly had the echoes of the clash with Britain died down when, in 1810, the struggle for independence from Spain began its long and tortuous course. Again the nascent patriotism found literary expression, this time in great abundance. The same López y Planes was one of the busiest bards celebrating victories and generally promoting patriotism. His outstanding work was a "Patriotic March" (1813). Set to music by a Catalan music teacher living in Buenos Aires and promptly given official endorsement by the Constituent General Assembly, it still remains the national anthem of Argentina. Another noted member of this group was Juan Cruz Varela, who like most of the rest, was a *porteño,* or native of Buenos Aires. He is generally adjudged a better poet than the others, but his themes were the same. Nearly everything he wrote celebrated the patriot heroes and their victories, or excoriated the Spanish tyrants, or proclaimed the future greatness of "the Argentine Republic," "triumphant, respected by the ambitious, free, rich, tranquil, organized."

As soon as the struggle with Spain was well over, these and other poems of the same kind were assembled and published by the government in a volume entitled *La lira argentina* (*The Argentine Lyre*). The first book of poetry ever published in Argentina, it was designed to promote patriotism and unity in a country threatened with civil war and disruption on the morrow of emancipation.

This little volume of verse, and other patriotic productions, official and private, of these early years, form what Ezequiel Martínez Estrada has called the "patristic literature" of Argentina's "canonical nationalism."[1] They did in fact determine the character of Argentine nationalism as it was to remain with little alteration for nearly a hundred years. Its basis was a patriotism expressed in terms borrowed mainly from France of the Revolution, but also from other countries, including even Spain. According to Martínez Estrada, patriotism was converted almost at once into nationalism, "that is to say," he explains, "into a cult of glory."

Since the canon had so long a life and though now greatly altered in some respects still stands in others, its character and content will repay examination.

The canon consists of two main parts. One is the so-called *doctrina de Mayo,* or "doctrine of May," which takes its name from the fact that the first step towards

Argentine independence was taken in May of 1810. Actually, however, the term denotes a corpus of official and private pronouncements by the country's founding fathers in the whole period from that date until independence was at last formally declared in July, 1816. The doctrine was forged in a politically confused period of trial and error during which Argentina moved slowly and hesitantly on the path towards independence. Nevertheless, as a recent writer has said,[2] the manifold expressions of Argentine thought in this period showed a high degree of agreement on such basic principles as popular sovereignty, liberty, equality, and fraternity, and on the need for popular education, freedom of speech, and separation of powers. Significantly, the same writer notes another agreed proposition: "The sense of forming part of a social organism, both materially and spiritually, assures coordination of efforts and cohesion in conduct. All this, developed into patriotism, will assure the felicity of all." Here were the makings of liberal nationalism.

The other part of the canon comprises literary works in the same tradition. The first important work of this kind was The Argentine Lyre, already mentioned. This was the voice of the first generation. The second is represented by a volume of poems, Consuelos, published a decade later (1834) by Esteban Echeverría. Founder of the romantic movement in Argentina and champion of "Young Argentina" (la joven Argentina), Echeverría was one of his country's most influential writers in the nineteenth century. In this and later works, notably his Dogma socialista (1846), Echeverría completed the "patristic canon" of Argentine nationalism on the basis of what he called "the portents of May." He reaffirmed its liberal, progressive, democratic character, and defended this against the reaction represented by Rosas.[3] Perhaps most important of all, he stressed its integrative function. In answer to the question, how the ideals of May were to be realized, he declared: "By means of the organization of liberty, fraternity, equality; by means of democracy. Resolve the problem of organization and you will resolve the problem of May."[4]

Martínez Estrada holds this "canonical nationalism" in low esteem, for a variety of reasons: because it was an artificial creation based on imported ideas; because it was the work of "official" writers and the literary salon; because it fails to express the feelings of the Argentine common people, including the gauchos (which he thinks were much better expressed by Juan Manuel de Rosas, whereas the canon condemns Rosas as an anti-Argentine tyrant); and because it deforms Argentina's reality, past and present, to produce a Utopian picture of its future that serves as a psychological crutch to the Argentine middle classes.

These are only a few samples of Martínez Estrada's philippic against Argentina's "canonical nationalism" as thus established, but they must suffice. Three comments on his philippic are in order.

In the first place, it is perfectly true, but not at all surprising, that Argentina's early nationalism was in almost every respect a faithful copy of the European prototype. The basis in popular sovereignty was the same. There was the same effort to give the national myth deep roots in the past. There was also the same cult of glory. National heroes were manufactured overnight, and a national anthem (still in use today) was composed and adopted even before Argentina declared its independence.

Sometimes the European models were copied with more fidelity than sense of proportion. In developing the cult of glory, for example, the Argentine poets of this period had their country's trumpet sounding from pole to pole and starting all America on the road to freedom, while "the nations" (presumably all the nations of the world) hearkened in amazement to "the portents of May" that proceeded from the infant republic of the Plata. What is more, the copyists reproduced Europe's forms of expression as well as basic ideas. The Argentine national anthem contains echoes of both the French *Marseillaise* and a patriotic Spanish song written in 1811 by Gaspar Melchor de Jovellanos. And, until the importation of literary romanticism brought about a change of models in the 1830's, almost all the patriotic poets of the Plata faithfully echoed the neoclassicism of their Spanish contemporaries in metrical forms, figures of speech, and vocabulary. The new heroes of Argentina were bracketed with Achilles, Alexander the Great, and Hannibal, and did not suffer by comparison.

Whatever one may think of all this, it was only to be expected. Argentina's whole literary culture, as well as the nationalist idea itself, was derived from Europe. And if the fervor of national pride seems to have been overdone at times, it should be remembered that no new nation's founders had greater need of a strong nationalist cement than those of Argentina. Their effort to give the new nation the broad dimensions of the colonial Viceroyalty of Buenos Aires was threatened from the start by particularisms that not only led to the early loss of Paraguay, Bolivia, and Uruguay, but also delayed the effective union of the remainder for more than half a century.

In the second place, while it cannot be denied, one must qualify the charge that this patristic nationalism was only the expression of a minority—a government clique, a literary salon such as Echeverría's—and not the voice of the Argentine people at large. For one thing, their voice was not wholly muted. One of the chief poets of these early years, Bartolomé Hidalgo, an Uruguayan, spoke for the gauchos, or cowboys, who were perhaps the most numerous group among the Argentine masses; politically, they were without question the most important for they were the chief prop of the dictatorship set up by Juan Manuel de Rosas in the 1830's. For another, the generally artificial and even stilted style of much of the literary production of nationalism in this period should not be permitted to blind us to the fact that it expressed, though in a distorted way, a feeling or sentiment that was genuine and widespread. This was the Americanism which had been taking shape in the Plata area, as in other European dominions in America, since the sixteenth century; which was everywhere a chief motive force of the independence movement; and which, as the general sentiment came to a focus on a particular geographical area, provided the basis for nationalism. Finally, the form, tone, and content of Argentina's early nationalist literature were determined by the nature of the task at hand. This was to influence the political activists; these were at first judged to be the social and intellectual elite, and to them, educated as they had been, there was nothing strange or stilted about this literature. The mistake the nationalist spokesmen made was in failing to perceive the strength of Rosas and his gauchos, who for a time diverted Argentina into a reactionary nationalism.

In these circumstances it would have been remarkable if Argentine nationalism had developed otherwise than as it did. The very fact that its canon, as established in the early years of national independence, remained unchanged so long seems good prima facie evidence that it met with the approval of the great bulk of Argentina's political activists at that time.

- Argentina - unlike Rest of
LA - which has had a
changing Face of
nat'lm - as noted earlier.

My third observation grows out of the one just made. It is that this canonical nationalism was not only primarily political but also politically liberal. It was likewise introspective, and, as regards other nations, benevolent and pacific. Argentina shared these traits with the Europe of the first half of the nineteenth century, and retained them long after they had been altered or reversed in Europe. To be sure, practice often failed to measure up to principle, as in the cases of Rosas's tyranny at home and long intervention in Uruguay, and of Argentina's participation in the Paraguayan War of 1864-1870. But then Rosas did not profess the principle he violated and did not in any case represent Argentina's dominant tradition. As for the Paraguayan War, Argentina at least began this as a war for the liberation of an oppressed people and at its end proclaimed the rule that "victory does not create rights." And Bartolomé Mitre, president of Argentina at that time, was some seventy years ahead of Herbert Hoover and Franklin Roosevelt in committing his country to the "good neighbor" policy.

3. Only the highlights of the further development of Argentina's canonical nationalism in the nineteenth century can be noted here. The first was its displacement by the reactionary nationalism of the Rosas regime, which started in 1829, was consolidated in 1835, and was overthrown in 1852. Brought to power with the aid of his gaucho following, Juan Manuel de Rosas was a prime example of the type of Latin American dictator euphemistically described by the Venezuelan Vallenilla Lanz as a "democratic Caesar." During most of his long rule, Rosas enjoyed widespread popular support; and, as is well known, he owed his popularity in considerable measure to his defense of Argentina for a dozen years

against French and British interventions which he deliberately helped to provoke for this purpose. He thereby appealed to one of the most primitive and powerful components of nationalist feeling, xenophobia.

What has less often been noted by foreign writers is that Rosas represented a reactionary type of nationalism in the broadest cultural sense. His was a reaction against the innovating cosmopolitanism of Bernardino Rivadavia, who had sought to transform Argentina culturally with French and British aid of many kinds, ranging from books and ideas to immigrants and capital investment. Rivadavia, too, was a nationalist, but his was an open, liberal nationalism of the canonical type: he wanted to make Argentina over into a new and better kind of nation with foreign aid. Rosas, on the other hand, defended the traditional, Spanish-based culture, but—and this is the important point—what he defended was Argentina's own creole variety of it. As for Mother Spain, he made no move towards reconciliation with her even in the cultural field, much less the political.

In short, the era of Rosas was marked by a rudimentary cultural nationalism. If we add the trait of aggressiveness so clearly manifested in his long intervention in Uruguay, it is clear that even at this early period Argentine nationalism was not only strong but fairly complex.

After Rosas's fall in 1852 liberal nationalism in Argentina revived and had a vigorous growth. In the next generation, under the leadership of such men as Bartolomé Mitre, Domingo Faustino Sarmiento, and Juan Bautista Alberdi, the tendencies of Rosas' brand of nationalism were reversed at almost every point. Cosmopolitanism once more prevailed, as it had under Rivadavia, only this time for a far longer period—for two thirds of a century, in fact. And, again as under Rivadavia, it was a kind of cosmopolitanism that was intended, not to weaken nationalism, but to strengthen the nation.

Again foreigners were invited to aid in many ways in the transformation of Argentine culture and society. Examples abound. Every schoolboy knows that the schoolteacher president of Argentina, Sarmiento, not only borrowed from the educational ideas and methods of Horace Mann of Massachusetts, but also imported a group of Yankee schoolmarms to put them into practice. Again, between the 1850's and World War I Argentina received more immigrants in proportion to its original population than any other country in the world, including the United States.

An even more striking illustration is the almost complete absence of economic nationalism in the post-Rosas generation. No better proof of its disappearance could be given than the fact that the constitution of 1853 not only authorized but directed the national government to foster foreign investments of private capital in Argentina (Article 67). The prescription was eagerly obeyed, particularly in regard to railway construction; and it is a noteworthy fact that, until the climate of opinion changed in the last decade of the century, under circumstances to be described below, the control of most of Argentina's railways by British and other foreign owners was seldom if ever objected to on nationalist grounds.

One of the best clues to the character of Argentine nationalism in the post-Rosas generation is provided by the fact that its chief exponent, Bartolomé Mitre, devoted his two major works to determining the origin and character of Argentine nationalism and that the central figures of these books were two fundamentally liberal soldier-statesmen, José de San Martín and Manuel Belgrano.[5]

After long and painstaking research in the documents,

Mitre concluded (as he had started by believing) that Argentine nationality antedated independence and that the nation was born democratic and liberal. In order to achieve self-expression, however, the Argentine people had first to throw off the Spanish yoke, which was relatively easy, and then to discover a satisfactory form of organization. The latter task, he recognized, was far more difficult, but, while details remained to be worked out, he believed that by the 1860's the quest had been substantially completed. The net impression conveyed by these and other works by Mitre was that Argentina was not only naturally a nation and naturally liberal-democratic but also now well on the way towards realizing the great destiny forecast for it by the poets and statesmen of the independence period. Thus Argentina's canonical nationalism achieved a new sanction, endorsement by the great Mitre. It was a powerful sanction, for by the last quarter of the century (and he lived until 1906) Mitre—general, president of the republic, owner and editor of a great newspaper, as well as the country's leading historian— had achieved the status of a father-figure in the minds of many Argentines.

In describing San Martín and Belgrano, Mitre did not use the term "liberal nationalists," but it fits his description of them like a glove. While both men were soldiers, neither was a militarist. On the contrary, both insisted on the subordination of the military to the civil authorities under a constitutional, firmly knit national government. As San Martín put it in an oft-quoted saying, "The army is a lion that must be kept in a cage and let out only on the day of battle."[6] Moreover, in the context of their times, the ideas of both men about the character of the civil government were relatively liberal— San Martín's monarchical propensities are no exception.

Their nationalism was likewise of a liberal cast as regards foreign relations. Both counseled a pacific, cooperative role, and endorsed interposition abroad only in the interest of extending the area of freedom—as San Martín tried to extend it in Chile and Peru, and Belgrano in Bolivia, and as Mitre himself at least proposed to do in Paraguay.

Our last highlight of the nineteenth century is the revival of economic nationalism that took place in its closing decade. This had already made a fleeting appearance under Rosas; now it came to stay. Since 1900 it has flourished until, in the last generation, it has become the most prominent single element, though not the strongest, in the whole complex of Argentine nationalism.

As already noted, Juan Bautista Justo, prestigious founder of the Socialist party in Argentina, was a leader in the movement for economic independence and dramatized the issue in words that moved Argentine national pride deeply. "What no foreign army could have achieved," he said, "has been accomplished by British economic penetration: the conquest of Argentina." By ringing many variations on this theme and driving it home tirelessly, year after year from the turn of the century on, the small but ably led Socialist party popularized it in Argentina. It was also taken up by the much larger Radical party and became the watchword of the country's first Radical President, Hipólito Irigoyen, elected in 1916.

But the theme was no monopoly of the parties of the left and center. As early as 1885 that pillar of the "oligarchy," Carlos Pellegrini, professed the conviction that "we must labor resolutely for our financial independence," since it was a sign of weakness and a reflection on the nation and its provinces that they had to turn to Europe even when they needed to raise only a few millions.[7] Pellegrini was likewise sure that the only way to win financial independence was by establishing "one large bank that will bring together all the credit resources and economic strength of the nation." Shortly after the revolt of 1890 and the economic crisis that helped to bring it about, Pellegrini had the satisfaction of playing the leading part in establishing such a bank. The same crisis marked a turning point in the public attitude towards foreign ownership of the great bulk of Argentina's railways. More and more this foreign hold came to be regarded as incompatible with the nation's dignity and independence.

Moreover, in the early years of the present century, shortly after the discovery of promising oil fields in the Comodoro Rivadavia area of Argentina, the first of a series of laws was passed to keep them from falling into foreign hands. This was the work of a conservative government controlled by the so-called oligarchy, as was also the act of 1936 which put the capstone on the petroleum legislation by establishing that chief symbol of Argentine economic nationalism, the government oil monopoly known as Yacimientos Petrolíferos Fiscales (YPF).

4. The new wave of Latin American nationalism set in motion by the centennial celebrations of independence in and about 1910 finds one of its best exemplars in Argentina, and no Argentine writer was a more articulate exponent of it than Ricardo Rojas, often called his country's "prince of letters." In the end, Rojas modified the canon of Argentine nationalism substantially. That he did so is hardly surprising, for the canon was largely a product of Buenos Aires, whereas he was a provincial, born and brought up in the back country, at Santiago del Estero, and ever loyal to it, though he moved to Buenos Aires at an early age and lived most of his life

there. It was one of his favorite theses that true Argentinism had its earliest and strongest roots in the interior provinces rather than in Buenos Aires.

Rojas's main ideas on nationalism were stated in three of his earliest works. The first, published in 1909, was *La restauración nacionalista* (*The Nationalist Restoration*). In 1910, the centenary of Argentina's first step towards independence, he followed this up with *Blasón de plata*,[8] which has been called an epic of the struggle for independence. In 1916, the centenary of Argentina's formal declaration of independence, he completed what we may call his trilogy of Argentine nationalism with a book whose main title is simply *La argentinidad*, or *Argentinity*.

The immediate problem dealt with in Rojas's first book was the teaching of history in Argentine schools, and when he went abroad in search of material for it he concentrated his attention on the teaching of history in selected foreign countries, principally Great Britain, France, Germany, Italy, Spain, and the United States. Nevertheless, he gave the completed work a broad sweep that fully justified its ambitious title, *The Nationalist Restoration*. What is more, this book adumbrated most of the ideas on Argentine nationalism that Rojas was to develop in the long remainder of his life.

In view of his conception of the problem and his scale of values, it was only natural that Rojas should have ended up by giving such broad dimensions to a study that began with so circumscribed a subject as the teaching of history in the schools. Basic to this book (and to his later books as well) was the conviction that, while politically independent ever since 1810, Argentina was not only still colonial, but had become increasingly colonial, in both its cultural and economic life. He further believed that these cultural and economic aspects of Argentine colonialism were closely related to each other and that they had a common origin in an Argentine disease which he labeled "cosmopolitanism." In his view, the enslavement of the Argentine people by foreign capital and their subservience to foreign ideas were twin expressions of a cosmopolitanism that had led to "a breakdown of the old moral nucleus, indifference to public affairs, increasing forgetfulness of traditions, the corruption of the language . . . lack of national unity."[9] And where did this cosmopolitanism in turn have its source? In Argentina's own schools, which had injected its poison into generation after generation of Argentine youth, until at last the whole body politic was infected. Hence the "nationalist restoration" must begin in the schools, and above all in the teaching of history, which must be purged of cosmopolitanism and put to patriotic uses. How this was to be done the book showed at great length.

In some respects *The Nationalist Restoration* marks Rojas as a continuator of Argentina's canonical nationalism, but in other respects he broke sharply with it. Like Mitre and other early molders of the canon, he regarded democracy as not only an essential but a primordial element of Argentine nationalism. Yet in his zeal for promoting the latter he was prepared, as Mitre never had been, to sacrifice the individual freedoms associated in the canon with democracy. Thus among the foreign systems of teaching history that Rojas examined, the one he admired most was the German, in which, he noted enviously, the teachers were "soldiers of a single national inspiration" and the schools were "forges of nationality." Leaving nothing to the imagination in this matter, he categorically rejected the claims of academic freedom (*libertad de enseñar*) as advanced by a noted contemporary, Joaquín V. González, who adhered to the canon in this respect. No, objected Rojas; when each teacher is free to present his own version of history, the resultant chaos endangers "the stability of the state" and "the moral integrity of the republic." Accordingly, he concluded that the national government must control education and create a community of ideas in order to "restore the national spirit . . . and save the Argentine school from the foreign clergy, from foreign gold, and from foreign books."[10]

The reference in the passage just quoted to "foreign clergy" only accentuates the note of secular nationalism that had been present in Argentina from the start, though latent much of the time and seldom dominant. On the other hand, a comparatively new note is struck in the next phrase, and a still newer one in the phrase that follows. "Foreign gold," of course, associates Rojas with the rising tide of economic nationalism in Argentina, but it also differentiates him from the canonical nationalists of the nineteenth century. Whereas they had welcomed foreign investments and business enterprise, which were the crux of the question, Rojas, as already noted, now complained that the Argentine people were being increasingly enslaved by foreign—particularly British—capital. He was to return to this theme time and again in subsequent works.

Rojas's most striking deviation from the nineteenth-century canon, however, is suggested by his sounding the tocsin against "foreign books." His notion that, in order to restore the national spirit, Argentina's schools (and her people at large) must be saved from foreign books and foreign ideas, sets him poles apart from all the canonical writers, and most of all from Sarmiento, whom he greatly admired in most respects. The break was quite conscious and deliberate on Rojas's part. Controverting the central thesis of Sarmiento's classic, *Facundo,* that the basic conflict in Argentina was one between civilization (the city) and barbarism (the countryside dominated by gauchos and caudillos), Rojas averred that the truly crucial conflict, on which the future of Argentine nationalism depended, was the one between *indianismo,*[12] or what is rooted and native, and *exoticismo,* or what is foreign and imported. This, too, is a recurrent theme in his later works, from the very next one, *Blasón de plata,* to his biography of Sarmiento, *El profeta de la pampa,* published more than thirty years later.[13]

Rojas laid no claim to originality for his attack on cosmopolitanism in Argentine education. On the contrary, he pointed out that similar attacks had been made by various ministers of public instruction, beginning in the 1860's. But they had gone unheeded and he felt it incumbent upon himself to take up the cudgels for nativism in the hope that through better publicity and greater persistence he would obtain better results before it was too late. Although the first reception of *The Nationalist Restoration* was disappointing, in the end his hope was justified. This was partly due to a favorable change in the climate of opinion under the impulse both of the nationalist fervor fired by the centennial celebration of independence and of the rise of the cult of the romanticized gaucho, who, once the butt of canonical nationalism, now became for many Argentines a symbol of nativism and the new nationalism. But Rojas's own persistence, combined with uncommon literary skill, contributed greatly to his success. The other two works in his trilogy, appearing in rapid succession, hammered his theme home, with suitable variations. With the publication of the third, *La argentinidad,* in 1916, Rojas was well established as the chief exponent of an Argentine nationalism that was both old and new, and more deeply rooted in Argentine experience and sentiment than the old.

Of the other two works in the Rojas trilogy, only *La argentinidad* calls for further comment. As indicated by its subtitle,[11] it deals directly with the formation of Argentina's "national consciousness" during the struggle for independence. Admittedly a work of imagination as well as historical research, it tells us even more about its twentieth-century author's idea of Argentine nationalism than about the ideas of his fellow countrymen on the same subject a century earlier. As clearly as his first book, though with the same modifications, *La argentinidad* stamps Rojas as belonging to the tradition of liberal nationalism. That is to say, he depicts Argentina's vital tradition as a liberal one, and Argentine nationalism as a beneficent force working for the unification of a free people at peace with its neighbors. *Argentinidad,* or "Argentinity," he says, is "that harmonious force . . . which impels us to the completion of our independence and the full realization of democracy." As this passage shows, he was not satisfied with what had been achieved in the past hundred years; indeed, he categorically asserts elsewhere that "we are still a colony" and deeply divided in many ways. But the dominant note is one of optimism. "Democracy," he concludes, "was the true fruit of *argentinidad*" in the struggle for independence, and the tradition thus established is being carried on by our more progressive political parties today.[14]

So far so good; but in this book Rojas was addressing himself mainly to the internal affairs of Argentina. In later years he gave more thought to his country's external relations, and in this context his affiliation with liberal nationalism is less clear. The element of xenophobia implicit in his assault on cosmopolitanism became more pronounced. Even Spain was not exempt from it, despite his personal ties with Spanish intellectuals and his admiration for certain aspects of Spanish culture, which, from the 1890's to the 1930's, flowered as never before since its *siglo de oro,* or Golden Age, three centuries earlier. Economic nationalism, too, loomed larger in his later writings, as did his thesis that foreign economic imperialism and Argentina's own cultural cosmopolitanism were twin aspects of the major threat to the integrity of *argentinidad.* And, it may be added, he came to regard the United States as a major source of the threat in both its aspects. Since, in domestic affairs, he remained a liberal nationalist to the end of his life in 1957, one might think that he should therefore have been more sympathetic towards the United States, the chief power among the democracies. Why he, and other Latin American nationalists like him, have not been so will be suggested in the next chapter.

To round out the picture, reference must be made to four of Ricardo Rojas's contemporaries who represent other aspects of Argentine nationalism as it developed before Perón gave it a new twist in the 1940's. One was Leopoldo Lugones, who was mainly responsible for making the vernacular gaucho poem *Martín Fierro* the chief symbol of "Argentinity" for a nation to whom the long-extinct gaucho now represented nothing but nostalgia. As a result, *Martín Fierro* became a classic example both of escapism and of the folk component of nationalism. Another representative was Carlos Ibarguren, a leader in the rehabilitation of Argentina's "democratic Caesar" of the nineteenth century, the tyrant Rosas. This Rosas cult gained strength from the popularity of *Martín Fierro,* for the hero of that bit of fabricated folklore was a defender of "the old order of things" which many Argentines associated with a romanticized Rosas.

The third member of this group was Manuel Gálvez, who resembled Ricardo Rojas in many ways but whose nationalism took a fascist turn in the 1930's.[15] Like Rojas, Gálvez was born in Argentina's back country, regarded it as the repository of true "Argentinity" and Buenos Aires as an alien bridgehead, assailed cosmopolitanism, North Americanization, and Europeanization, and yet was strongly influenced by foreign writers, beginning with the Spanish "Generation of 1898." Also like Rojas, Gálvez was a *Martín Fierro* enthusiast and alternately praised Sarmiento and Mitre for their "Argentinity" and scolded them for their cosmopolitanism. And Gálvez, too, saluted Argentina's centenary of independence in 1910 with one of his earliest books, *El diario de Gabriel Quiroga: opiniones sobre la vida argentina,* which was the first of a long line of works (mostly novels) aimed at promoting the revitalization of Argentine nationalism.

Unlike Rojas, Gálvez was at first reluctant to use the term "nationalism" (to which he preferred "traditionalism"), but accepted it because it was so well established. Once he had adopted it, he promoted it with exemplary vigor. Defining it as "nothing but militant patriotism," he carried militancy to the point of urging that Argentina declare war on Brazil, not for conquest but, on the contrary, in the expectation that Argentina would be defeated and that the defeat would provide the national catharsis necessary for the resurgence of true nationalism.

For the most part, however, Gálvez's nationalism was less bellicose than this proposal might suggest; indeed, he insisted that aggressiveness was one of the chief flaws in the Argentine national character, and must be curbed. He had a more definite program than did Rojas and most other nationalists of that period. The program was to be carried out partly by such measures as the promotion of education, economic development, and the assimilation of Argentina's horde of immigrants. In the latter connection, alluding to the famous nineteenth-century phrase in which Juan Bautista Alberdi had summed up the half-vacant country's need for immigrants, "To govern is to people," Galvez said, "Nowadays, to govern is to Argentinize." Another way in which he proposed to carry out his program was by borrowing from abroad, for neither his anti-cosmopolitanism nor his traditionalism was absolute. Discussing this question in another book, in 1913, he said: "Two political tendencies exist in my country. The first [is] conservative and in a certain sense traditionalist and regressive. . . . The second tendency is cosmopolitan and liberal . . . it looks too much towards Europe and the United States; it wants progress at any cost. . . . The latter has recently been called *progressive nationalism*, while the former, which is the true nationalism, has been styled *historical*. I believe that these two tendencies should be united in one."[16]

Perhaps it was in this eclectic spirit that, some two decades later, Gálvez turned to fascist Europe for inspiration. By this time events had raised a serious question about the aptitude of the Argentine people for political democracy. In 1930 the constitutional government headed by President Hipólito Irigoyen had been ousted by a military revolt. Next came a dictatorship and after that an oligarchy; and all the while Argentina suffered from the world-wide economic depression. In these circumstances, in 1934, Gálvez published a book, *Este pueblo necesita* (*What This People Needs*) in which he urged his fellow countrymen to scrap their made-in-U.S.A. constitution and set up an authoritarian government of the type represented by Mussolini's Italy and Hitler's Germany. The best that can be said for this proposal is that it was Gálvez's prescription for achieving social justice and national greatness. In 1940 he topped this off with a novelized and sympathetic biography of Rosas which proved "vastly popular."[17]

The fourth and last member of our representative group was the Irigoyen mentioned above, of whom we shall have more to say in the next section.

5. Reference has already been made to the growth of economic nationalism in Argentina from the late nineteenth century on. Its development was gradual and will be difficult to correlate with the history of social change in the same period until both processes have been investigated much more closely than hitherto. As matters now stand, one can only venture two working hypotheses, both rather vague. The first is that until 1916 the domination of Argentina by an "oligarchy" who had a large stake in foreign trade and close ties with foreign investments checked the development of such nationalist manifestations as threatened to injure those interests by upsetting Argentina's foreign relations. The curb applied with special force to economic nationalism. The second hypothesis is that the gradual emergence of economic nationalism despite this curb can be attributed mainly to the parallel growth of the middle class, which achieved considerable influence in the quarter-century before 1916, although ultimate control still remained in the hands of the oligarchy.

In contrast with that earlier period, economic nationalism has burgeoned more rapidly in Argentina since 1916 and can be correlated more closely with social and political change.[18] It has done much to shape the course

of every one of the highly diversified regimes that have
governed Argentina since 1916. To begin with, the left-
wing Radical administration of Hipólito Irigoyen an-
nounced the theme of economic nationalism in clarion
tones and stated it in still classic terms. Briefly, Irigoyen
linked economic independence, which to him meant an
anti-imperialism directed mainly against Great Britain
and the United States, with social transformation, which
in turn involved an attack on Argentina's own oligarchy;
and he coupled the two by branding the oligarchs as
vendepatrias, people who had sold control of their country to foreigners for their own enrichment. Similar ideas
underlay the Mexican Revolution of 1910, but in Argentina they were not carried to the same extreme, for despite
their label the Radicals in Argentina were essentially a
middle-class party and hardly more radical than the contemporary Wilson Democrats in the United States. This
was true even of Irigoyen's left wing of the party, and still
more so of his successor Alvear's right wing. Moreover,
the two wings split, the middle class lost coherence as it
grew in numbers, and Radicalism became impotent just
when a national crisis demanded strong action.

In 1930, at the first onset of the great depression,
the Radical government, again headed by Irigoyen after
an overwhelming victory at the polls in 1928, was ousted
by a military coup amidst general public applause. For
our purposes, the revolution of 1930 is significant for two
reasons. First, the Radicals' disaster was due in large
part to the failure of these economic nationalists to defend
the nation's economy in the current crisis, for Irigoyen,
now decrepit but still dominant, had sat with folded arms
while the economy of the richest country in Latin America went to pot. In the second place, this revolution
marks the emergence of Argentina's armed forces in the

role of final arbiter of the nation's political disputes—a role which they have continued to play ever since. While the armed forces have never formed a monolithic bloc and have at times been split wide open—most obviously in the short but sharp civil war that ended in Perón's overthrow in 1955—their various factions nevertheless have one thing in common: they are all nationalists of one kind or another. As a result, their achievement of a decisive role in public affairs has strengthened the nationalist component in Argentine policy and public opinion in the past thirty years.

After a brief interval of military dictatorship in 1930-1931, the oligarchy returned to power for a decade under a conservative coalition, known as the *Concordancia,* with the tacit support of the military. Yet it was now a changed oligarchy—changed most in its respect for economic nationalism. This had become so strong a force that it could not in any case have been ignored, and it was strengthened by several developments in this decade. For one thing, these depression years promoted nationalism in most of the Western world, and Argentina was no exception. For another, in Argentina nationalism in the particular form of autarky was stimulated by fascist influences playing on that country from the Italy of Mussolini, the Germany of Hitler, and the Spain of Franco. Again, the oligarchy itself was modified by the rapid growth of industry, which clamored for protection. Perhaps most important of all was the influence of the military, which we have just noted. Partly because their largest and politically strongest group, the army officers, were German-trained, the military were even more nationalistic in this decade and the next than the middle class from which most of these Argentine officers have come.

As a result, the restored oligarchy could not have reverted wholly to its earlier economic liberalism even if it had wanted to. In fact, its motives were mixed, and so was its record. On the one hand, its Roca-Runciman agreement of 1933, sacrificing Argentina's manufactures to her ties with Great Britain, was like a voice from the past. On the other hand, present and future spoke in the completion of the YPF oil monopoly and in other measures, such as the tightening of controls over the foreign-owned *frigoríficos,* which in the next decade provided the arch-economic-nationalist Perón with a good base to build on.

Juan Perón made two outstanding contributions to the development of economic nationalism during his twelve years in power (the last nine, 1946-1955, as president). Together, these crowned the work begun by Irigoyen a generation earlier. The first was Perón's formal "Declaration of Economic Independence" in 1947. Made on the anniversary of Argentina's declaration of political independence of 1816, and at the same place, this dramatized the issue as perhaps nothing else could have done, and fixed the achievement of economic independence irrevocably (at least in the minds of most Argentines) as a major objective of public policy. Second, and even more important, Perón revolutionized the social implications of economic nationalism by identifying it with social revolution for the benefit of the Argentine underdogs, the *descamisados.* Irigoyen had adumbrated this identification, but Perón formulated and achieved it.

To be sure, Perón's achievement was purely verbal. For reasons that we cannot stop to examine, he failed to carry out the promised social revolution, and towards the end he even retreated from economic nationalism. But the fact that his failure and his retreat did more than anything else to bring about his overthrow only shows how successful he had been in indoctrinating the Argentine masses with his new version of economic nationalism—new at least in Argentina.

Further evidence to the same effect has been provided by the course of events since Perón's fall, and especially since the beginning of the administration of President Arturo Frondizi on May 1, 1958. In December of that year he surprised most Argentines and shocked many by adopting an ambitious but austere stabilization-and-development plan backed by the International Monetary Fund and the United States government. Competent economists regard this plan as not only sound but indispensable to the long-range welfare of the Argentine people at large, and so far it has worked well. Yet it quickly aroused such widespread resentment that Frondizi's party was routed in the next national election (1960) and, subsequently, in several provincial or local elections. The opposition to his plan rests on two main grounds. The first is that it is based on a liberal economic policy that the Argentine majority has been taught to associate with the alleged corrupt alliance formed by the *vendepatria* oligarchy with foreign "imperialists" at the expense of the rest of the nation. Frondizi has even let foreigners lay their profane hands on that sacred cow of economic nationalists, Argentina's oil industry. Secondly, the plan imposed austerity with a promise of benefits, but yielded benefits at too slow a rate to satisfy the Argentine masses. Like the masses in many other lands, they want to have a more abundant life *now* and are impatient for the social tranformation promised them by Perón—and also by Frondizi, when he was running for president.

While Frondizi has purged Argentine nationalism of some of its excesses, its hold on him and the nation at

*argentine
cultures are*
↑ *wrong* — *Friedly was
not struggling from
[illegible] politicals.*

large seems as firm as ever. He was never more the
nationalist than when accepting the guidance of the International Monetary Fund or inviting foreign private capital
to invest in Argentina, for by such measures he sought to
bring about the economic development which he regarded
as an indispensable prerequisite to the establishment of
true national sovereignty. "No backward country," he
declared in 1961, "is fully independent." His nationalism was not exclusively economic; in the same address he
reaffirmed Argentina's traditional adherence to "the three
basic principles" of the juridical equality of states, nonintervention, and self-determination.[19]

This was still the mood of the Argentine nation, too.
A straw in the wind was a book made up of articles originally published in 1960 in connection with the sesqui-
centennial celebration of Argentina's political independence. It bore the eloquent title "Argentina a World
Power."[20] Again, as in 1910, the anniversary evoked,
not only affirmations of national pride, but assertions that
national independence was still incompletely established,
and prescriptions for achieving it. The difference was
that the chief source of weakness was now identified with
economic underdevelopment rather than with cosmopolitanism. Hence the book dealt mainly with such matters
as increased steel and power production, more and better
roads, and improved agricultural methods. But the author
looked back as well as forward, invoking the national
anthem, the spirit of May, and "the dream of 1810,
which has still to be realized." Calling on that "awakened
giant," the Argentine people, to tone up its muscles, he
cried: "Together, let us put our shoulders to the task of
the Imperative National Priority: *Argentina a World
Power.*"

6. Economic nationalism has been featured in this sketch of Argentine developments since Irigoyen's advent to power in 1916 because it has been the most prominent of all the constant or recurrent themes of the period. Two qualifications, however, must be added: the first is that, in Argentina as elsewhere, all forms of nationalism, including the economic, are at bottom political; the second, that Argentine nationalism found abundant expression in non-economic terms as well during these years. Both points are illustrated by the fact that although the nationalism headlined by Perón was economic, the national hero whom he sought to appropriate as the symbol of his regime was the liberator José de San Martín, a historic figure rich in military and political associations but devoid of any economic significance whatsoever. Another example is the development of an aggressive nationalism that expressed itself, both before and during the Perón period, in a bid for Argentine hegemony, at least in the Plata basin or the area of the old Viceroyalty of Buenos Aires, and sometimes even more widely. Still another example is the peculiar attachment of Argentina to the nationalistic doctrine of absolute nonintervention.

Argentina's devotion to this doctrine had its roots in the nineteenth century but reached full flower in the period after 1916. It also had ramifications of various kinds, such as the neutralism of Irigoyen, the Third Position of Perón, and the anti-Pan-Americanism, which, in the sense of Latin Americanism, enjoyed a considerable vogue in Argentina in the early years of independence. Though subsquently weakened, first by the near chaos into which most of Latin America fell for a time, and then by the sharp disparity that developed between Argentina and most of the rest of Latin America through large-scale European immigration and rapid economic development, Latin Americanism never completely died out among the Argentines. Recently, it has even revived somewhat, as various developments have reduced the disparity. That the revival will continue may be doubtful, but the possibility should not be ruled out. Among the considerations in its favor is the fact that, to the tradition-conscious Argentines, José de San Martín is a symbol not only of their nationalism but also, however paradoxically, of a broad Latin Americanism.

The next chapter will seek to resolve this paradox by considering Latin Americanism as a form of extended or continental nationalism. But the focus will shift to other countries, where the phenomenon is more highly developed than in Argentina.

Continental
Nationalism
and the U.S.

1. Alongside the conventional kind of nationalism—
that associated with a single country—another
variety is currently engaging the attention of some of
Latin America's leading writers. Although it usually goes
under the paradoxical name of continental nationalism,
its meaning is clear: it connotes a synthesis of the nation-
alisms of the individual Latin American countries. The
noted Peruvian writer and political leader Víctor Raúl
Haya de la Torre has a more evocative term for it: *la
patria grande,* the "great fatherland."

For historians the current vogue of continental nationalism has the charm of antiquity, since the *patria grande*
concept not only has roots in the past but is in essence
only a revival of an idea as old as Latin American independence. For students of current affairs the phenomenon gains significance from the fact that it is by no
means peculiar to Latin America. It is exhibited likewise

in the oldest area of modern nationalism, Western Europe, as well as in its newest area, Africa, where leaders of the new states just coming off the nationalist assembly line are already seeking to merge them in a Pan African union. For all interested students this combination of durability in Latin America with contemporary parallels in other areas entitles the *patria grande* ideal to serious consideration despite the enormous obstacles—chief among which is conventional nationalism—that stand in the way of its fulfillment.

The present chapter will first sample historical antecedents and current expressions of the idea of continental nationalism in Latin America. It will then weigh the factors working for or against the practical application of the idea. Finally, it will consider the implications of both this and the conventional form of Latin American nationalism for the United States.

2. Vain but valiant efforts were made by many of Latin America's founding fathers to give the whole area some kind of political unity. From that time to the end of the century such efforts were confined very largely to Spanish America, but they prepared the way for the broader Latin Americanism that began to take shape early in the present century.[1]

The story of the first phase of Spanish Americanism is a familiar one. No account, however brief, of the emergence of these new states fails to cite the outstanding example of the South American liberator, Simón Bolívar, and his best-known contributions to the cause of unification: his Jamaica Letter of 1815 and the Panama Congress of 1826. For our purposes, however, the Chilean[2] Juan Egaña is an even better exponent of the idea. That Egaña's advocacy of the cause began several years before Bolívar's is less important than that he advocated it with fewer reservations and in terms that echoed even more faithfully the nationalism produced in Europe by the French Revolution.

Charged by the Chilean patriots' first national congress in 1811 with drafting a constitution for the new state, Egaña produced a document which called Chile a "people" and reserved the term "nation" for a union of Chile with the other free peoples of Spanish America. In this sense Article II of his draft provided that "the people of Chile" should retain control of their foreign relations pending the formation of "a general Congress of the nation, or the greater part thereof, or at least of South America (if the [inclusion] of the [whole] nation is not possible)," and the formation of "a general system of union and mutual security," whereupon Chile's reserved powers should be surrendered to the general Congress. While Egaña saw the need for mutual defense as the strongest bond of union in this continental nation, he also believed it would be held together by ties of "blood, language, interrelations, laws, customs, and religion."[3]

In later years, as nationalism crystallized in Chile and other countries, Egaña made some concessions to it in minor matters, but none of substance. In 1818, when Chile's independence was definitely established, he was ready to settle for its external sovereignty as well as its domestic autonomy, but on condition that it take the lead in persuading "the other governments of America" to create a "national or confederate sovereignty" of the whole and a single system of public law. Eight years later, in connection with the Panama Congress, he proposed the establishment of a "federation of the former Spanish colonies" as the best means of promoting mutual defense and a common system of public law; he even proposed to give the federation a measure of control over its members' commerce. Cooperation with the rest of free America, including the United States, was envisaged, but to the end his chief aim was to promote the union of the Spanish American states. And he never wavered in the belief that, while such a union was primarily needed for their security, they were also "naturally invited" to it by (as he put it in 1826) "their uniformity in language, religion, interests, customs, ideas and opinions."[4] This was at least a rudimentary form of continental nationalism.

Although even the less ambitious effort at union represented by the Panama Congress of 1826 failed, the underlying idea of a community of Latin American interest did not die out. It achieved a modest measure of political and legal expression in the next hundred years— notably in the conferences held at Lima in 1847 and 1865—despite the generally unfavorable character of developments, both domestic and foreign, during this period. Thus, in the first generation or two of independence the widespread prevalence of alternating anarchy and dictatorship was more propitious to further fragmentation than to union. Again, the establishment of independence was followed not by an increase but by a decline in travel and communication among the various parts of Latin America. This trend was aggravated by the impact of large-scale foreign investments and business enterprise, which—as noted with regard to Argentina in the preceding chapter—fostered disparities among the Latin American countries and increasingly oriented most of them away from their neighbors and towards Europe and the United States. It also fostered the "cosmopolitanism" to which the Argentines Ricardo Rojas and Manuel Gálvez took such strong exception and which was adverse not only to nationalism, as Rojas complained, but also to that sense of Latin American solidarity which provides the underpinning for continental nationalism. And finally, these developments tended to widen the gap that had always existed between the Spanish American states and the other two members of the Latin American group, Brazil and Haiti.

Since World War I a number of developments have brought about a limited but significant resurgence of this Latin American community sense. Reduced to its simplest terms, the explanation lies mainly in the deepening involvement of all Latin America in world affairs of many kinds—political, economic, cultural, and military. Closer association with the outside world, and particularly with the great powers, gave many Latin Americans a new perspective, in which their differences with and from one another were diminished and their resemblances magnified. It was brought home to them, as never before, that, though in varying degrees, all the Latin American countries were relatively weak, relatively poor, and both Latin (which set them off from the United States) and American (which set them off from Europe). The lesson was learned in a series of concrete situations, extending from the long controversy with the United States over intervention and the disaster of the depression decade after 1929 to the United States's preoccupation after World War II with Europe and Asia, which provoked a common Latin American complaint of neglect.

The period since World War I has also been marked by a vast improvement in the means of communication among the Latin American countries, above all through the development of radio and air transport. Deepening involvement in world affairs has had a similar effect by providing both opportunity and occasion for sustained group action on the part of the Latin American delegates to international gatherings. The prime example is the United Nations. Soon after its establishment, the Latin Americans formally organized themselves into a bloc which meets regularly and, while not monolithic, usually determines the votes of the great majority on key questions. They also induced the United Nations Economic and Social Council to set up an Economic Commission for Latin America (ECLA), which has played a significant role in formulating and disseminating Latin American views on the economic problems of that area.

The resurgence of Latin Americanism since World War I is apparent in other ways as well. Of the many examples that might be given, perhaps the most significant because of its growing importance relates to organized labor. The first general Latin America organization ever established in this field, the Latin American Confederation of Labor (CTAL), was created at Mexico City in 1938. Becoming tainted with Communism, it declined in the 1940's and was largely supplanted by the Organización Regional Interamericana de Trabajadores, a branch of the World Confederation of Free Trade Unions. Interestingly enough, that parent body was reluctant to approve organization on a regional basis, but was overborne by Latin American insistence. Also, while nominally inter-American, ORIT is essentially Latin American in composition and program. In addition, two efforts to set up labor organizations encompassing all Latin America have been launched by individual governments in that area: by the Argentina of Perón and, quite recently, by the Cuba of Fidel Castro. All these essays bespeak a recognition of the growing importance not only of Latin American labor but also of Latin Americanism itself.

3. It may, of course, be a very far cry from a more or less vague Latin Americanism to anything that merits the more specific label "continental nationalism." Let us therefore see what some of Latin America's own writers have had to say on the subject in recent years.

Precisely because its theme is not continental nationalism, a recent article by a noted Cuban writer, the late Jorge Mañach, gives striking expression to belief in the underlying unity of Hispanic America. Mañach's concern in this article is with the resemblances and differences between the latter and Spain. Hispanic America's own unity is taken for granted, as something that needs to be, not proved, but only described. He lists its three principal bonds of union as language, private customs, and public customs. Among the last named he includes a firm though often frustrated vocation for democracy. As he sums it up, there exist a common "psychological 'style' and a mode of behavior relatively characteristic of the Hispanic Americans, which make us feel and see ourselves as members of the same family and generically distinct from the North Americans and from most Europeans. . . ."[5]

Leopoldo Zea, a leading Mexican intellectual, has dealt with the political theme more directly. In 1957 he devoted a whole book to proving the need and viability of a *comunidad hispanoamericana,* a Hispanic American community.[6] To Zea the present multiple-state system is only a way station on the road to the merger of all the area's fragments in a single all-embracing whole. Writing in 1958 from another point of view, the Colombian Gustavo Correa found in the literary history of Latin America no important evidence of conventional nationalism and much convincing evidence of continental Latin Americanism.[7]

Two other recent writers have given the continental idea a quite explicit political application. One is Antenor Orrego, who, in an article entitled "Continental Nationalism," sketched his thesis in historical terms.[8] Towards the close of the colonial period, he declared, the people of Latin America developed, vaguely but firmly, a "continental sense of our destiny as a historical and spiritual whole, one and indivisible." At first the leaders of the new states acted in this sense, but soon the independence movement was perverted from its true purpose by selfish oligarchs and military leaders, who perpetuated the injustices and localisms of the old regime under the guise of a fragmented nationalism borrowed from Europe. To make matters still worse, in Spanish America the configuration of the new states slavishly followed that of the political subdivisions of the colonial period, and differed from it mainly in that nationalism further widened the artificial and frustrating gap between one subdivision and another.

Hence, according to Orrego, the present-day political map of the "independent" Latin American states is itself a vestige of colonialism. From this proposition it is but one step to his conclusion that, in order to complete their aborted independence movement, the Latin Americans must rediscover themselves by reviving continental nationalism—as, he believes, they are now at last doing. In his opinion this must be a continental nationalism devoted to freedom and justice, without distinction of race or creed, and must be placed at the service of all peoples everywhere.

Another writer who has recently given the idea an explicit political application is the Peruvian Aprista leader Víctor Raúl Haya de la Torre. Haya develops the thesis in less apocalyptic and more concrete terms than

Orrego, but bases it on a similar interpretation of history.[9]
"For me," declares Haya, "Latin America is the *Patria Grande*, of which each of its component states is an inseparable and interdependent part. I believe that the best patriotism for any Latin American with regard to the country of his birth is to sustain the inseparability of our states as members of a continental whole."

Haya, too, makes much of the prevalence of this concept of continental unity in the early years of independence, but he attributes the departure from it, not to a selfish oligarchy, but to mistaken judgment—the mistake made by the leaders of the post-Bolívar era in imitating the example of fragmented, nationalist Europe instead of that of the United States, which pooled its several state sovereignties in a federal union. In fragmented Latin America, on the other hand, nationalism became ever more pronounced and imitation of Europe was carried to such a point that the South American War of the Pacific (1879-1883)[10] was a sequel to the Franco-German war of 1870-1871. In developing his thesis Haya lays strong stress on economic factors, both as proof of the need for Latin American union and as a chief instrument for giving it substance—as, for instance, through the Economic Commission for Latin America and a Latin American common market.

4. How seriously should we take this call to Pan Latin American nationalism? Conventional nationalism is a formidable barrier to its growth, and its exponents have no agreed plan of action or blueprint of union. It is not even clear that they are all talking about the same thing, or even about the same geographical area. Again today, as in Bolívar's time, some of them are obviously thinking primarily if not exclusively of Spanish America

when they use such terms as "this continent" and "our America." Brazil and Haiti do not fit easily into the terms of most of the discourse on this subject.

Nevertheless, whatever the obstacles and whatever the exact extent of the contemplated area may be, the current wave of continental nationalism in Latin America merits careful consideration. As already noted, the phenomenon is not peculiar to Latin America. Rather, it is a part of a widespread trend—an almost world-wide trend—in response to the felt need for better protection in the hard-bitten world of today than the existing nation-states can offer. To some the obvious answer is world government, but the obstacles to achieving that in the visible future are so great, and the nationalist pattern of thought and feeling is so firmly fixed throughout the world, that others think the only practical remedy lies in mergers of kindred nations in a broader if not higher nationalism of continental scope.

Among all the current manifestations of this trend, the Latin American variety is not the least likely to thrive. Despite the great strength of conventional nationalism in Latin America, the obstacles to the development of the continental variety are less formidable there than in most other areas. Some of the Latin American "nations" still seem an artificial creation (Bolivia is a striking example), and most of them have become increasingly conscious that they are too weak to stand alone for long amidst the tensions of the present-day world. Conversely, the linguistic barriers to unity are far less formidable in Latin America than in most other comparable areas. Western Europe's diversity of Scandinavian, Germanic, and Romance languages is too familiar to need cataloguing here. Africa speaks a thousand languages, and in one state alone, Ghana, the five million inhabitants speak twenty vernaculars and its government is taking a short-cut when it broadcasts to them in only six languages. In Latin America, on the other hand, the great majority of its nearly 200 million inhabitants speak either Spanish or Portuguese, which are closely akin.

On the positive side, as already noted, Latin American continentalism possesses at least the rudiments of several traits associated with conventional nationalism. There is a sense of Latin American solidarity, widely though by no means universally held. This rests in part on a tradition as old as the Latin American nations themselves. There are also symbols of solidarity, chief among them Simón Bolívar, who, although identified in his lifetime with northern South America, has become the talisman of unity for all Spanish America. Even the Mexican Leopoldo Zea bases his case for a Hispanic American community squarely on what he calls "the Bolivarian ideal." Finally, efforts to give the continental idea practical expression have been made from the start and are not only being continued. In our own time they have been intensified under pressure from a shrinking world that threatens with destruction weak nations isolated and exposed by continued dalliance with conventional nationalism.

5. Now let us look at another aspect of the many-sided state of Latin American thought and feeling. The people of that area also have a related but quite different tradition, that of Western Hemisphere solidarity, which they share with the United States and which, for the sake of brevity and for lack of a better term, we may refer to as Pan Americanism. What is the bearing of this Pan American tradition on the current vogue of continental nationalism, or Pan Latin Americanism, of which

we have just been speaking? And how will each of these forces, or both together, affect the United States?

To begin with the former question, it appears that Pan Americanism and Pan Latin Americanism are not necessarily competitors, and may even be co-workers, so long as the character of the respective relationships connoted by them remains international. It will be otherwise, however, when either of them takes on the character of extended nationalism. That is just what Pan Latin Americanism is beginning to do, as is apparent from the alternative name by which it is now known, "continental nationalism." In such a contingency the two forces will certainly compete with each other. They may even become involved in headlong collision with each other as a result of the strain of xenophobia that is at least latent in all forms of nationalism.

The advantage in their competition for Latin American loyalty lies quite obviously with Pan Latin Americanism. It is true, as pointed out earlier, that there are many handicaps on the development of the latter as a form of extended nationalism; but, whether in this form or merely as a framework for international cooperation, Pan Americanism has to contend not only with all these handicaps, but with others as well.

That the handicaps of this kind extend from cultural diversity to clashing particularisms is so obvious that there is no need to labor the point. It might not be amiss, however, to note some of the indications that there is in fact an inclination among Latin Americans to draw away from the United States and together with one another, in a way that suggests the existence of a nascent continental naionalism militating against Pan Americanism.

This is not asserted here as a demonstrable—much less as a demonstrated—proposition, but only as a working hypothesis that deserves consideration. Most of the data for testing it will probably be found in the periods of international crisis of the past half-century, including the current ferment in Latin America. These data make a *prima facie* case for considering the hypothesis seriously. They suggest that a Pan Latin Americanism at odds with Pan Americanism has not only grown in the past half-century, but that it has gained widespread support from various sectors of Latin American society, right wing as well as left.

An impressive right-wing instance occurred two decades ago. This was the publication in Buenos Aires in 1941, two years after the beginning of World War II and only a few months before the Japanese attack on Pearl Harbor, of a book bearing the interrogative title *Hispano-América en guerra?* It was written by a Peruvian, Felipe Barreda Laos. An intellectual of some prominence, Barreda was a philosophical liberal. A few years earlier he had written an intellectual history of the Viceroyalty of Peru that excoriated the tyranny and obscurantism of Spain's colonial regime and celebrated the Peruvian creoles' struggle for enlightenment and freedom. Politically and socially, however, Barreda was conservative. When he wrote *Hispano-América en guerra?*, he was serving the right-wing Prado government as Peru's ambassador to both Argentina and Uruguay; hence its publication in Buenos Aires. His closest associates in those countries were, not surprisingly, people of his own and his government's kind—in Uruguay, the right-wing Herreristas and, in Argentina, the conservative coterie represented by Enrique Ruiz Guiñazú, who, like Barreda, was a historian and who became his neutralist government's minister of foreign affairs in June, 1941, just before Barreda's book appeared.

And what did this book have to say? It answered the

query of its title with a resounding "No!" The United States, Barreda charged, was not only embarked on a course that would obviously lead to its early entry into the world war as a belligerent, but was also making improper use of the inter-American system in a transparent effort to drag Latin America along with it into the war. That effort, he held, must be resisted at all costs, and his whole book was devoted to explaining why he was convinced the time had come for the peoples of Latin America to part company with the United States and develop their many common ties with one another into a more perfect union. In short, his book is a striking right-wing expression of a nascent continental nationalism in conflict with the Western Hemisphere idea of Pan American solidarity.

As for corresponding left-wing expressions, the most clear-cut of these in the past generation have come from Communist or fellow-traveler sources, and they appear in two phases. According to Víctor Alba,[11] a leading authority on communism in Latin America, the first phase covers roughly the 1930's and '40's. At that time, he tells us, Communist agents were very active in Latin America, especially in intellectual and labor circles, and they early made nationalism a favorite theme. They did so under the force of circumstances rather than deliberately, for no alternative theme was nearly so rewarding— the Nazi menace seemed remote in Latin America, and Roosevelt's Good Neighbor policy had taken the steam out of the anti-imperialist campaign, whereas nationalism always offers a fertile field. Accordingly, they cultivated it assiduously, but theirs was a negative, disruptive nationalism. While it served its purpose of fostering antagonism against the United States, it also tended to disrupt Latin America itself by setting each country not only apart from, but against, its neighbors.

Book written in 1962

6. Today we are in the second phase of left-wing Pan Latin Americanism. This began a few years ago, says Alba, and is marked by two principal traits. One is the return to a positive, humane nationalism whose primary concern is with the welfare of the individual. The other is the revival of the *conciencia americana* or sense of the Latin American community—its existence, its worth, its possibilities. To put it another way, this second phase is characterized by a combination of continental nationalism with populism.

Alba believes that this phase is also marked by a decline of Communist influence on the molding of Latin American nationalism. He may be right, but I am confident that any such decline has been more than offset by the rapid rise of Latin American populism. Since 1959 the latter has found its most conspicuous expression in Fidelismo—the policies, ideas, and attitudes represented by Fidel Castro's Cuba. Although Cuba's ties with the Communist bloc make it difficult to appraise the difference between the two, Fidelismo is probably a greater potential threat than communism to the interests of the United States in Latin America. This is because Fidelismo expresses so well the rising Latin American tide of both continental nationalism and populism. The blend is made all the more pleasing to many Latin American palates by its strong flavor of anti-imperialism and Yankeephobia, which have flourished again since the passing of Franklin Roosevelt and his Good Neighbor policy.

Perhaps the most important feature of Fidelismo is its appeal to Latin American nationalism in both the senses in which the term is used in these pages—both the conventional nationalism of the individual country and the extended, continental nationalism of Latin America at large. In the latter sense Fidelismo at the moment represents only an aspiration, but it is an aspiration that could quite conceivably achieve a substantial degree of realization. At first it aroused a highly favorable response among many Latin Americans of the center and left. More recently, however, this support has dwindled as Castro's affiliation with Communism has become unmistakable, for this offends the ingrained, almost instinctive, Americanism of most Latin Americans, whether their Americanism takes the form of conventional nationalism or of continental nationalism.

The cases of Mexico and Brazil are particularly instructive in this connection. They are also particularly important because these are so much the largest countries in Latin America that, together, they contain almost one half the total population of its twenty countries. Mexico, a stable country for the past generation and apparently inoculated against further extremism by its own Revolution of 1910, has shown few signs of welcoming Fidelismo for domestic consumption. Moreover, in August, 1960, Mexico joined in the Declaration of San José made by the Organization of American States against outside interference (meaning Soviet interference) in Western Hemisphere affairs. Yet Mexico promptly denied that this declaration was aimed at Castro's regime and declared its own warm sympathy with that regime's program of social and economic reform.

Early in 1961 Mexico reinforced this attitude, and gave more aid and comfort to Fidelismo, by permitting a pro-Castro Latin American congress to be held on Mexican soil. Mexico's attitude would seem to be that, although she has no need for Fidelismo herself, she thinks it would be a good thing for export to the other Latin American countries and will help them enjoy its benefits. Yet, this is coupled with unremitting hostility to non-

Latin-American interference in Latin American affairs. In short, Mexico's substantial weight is thrown behind the current trend towards continental nationalism *cum* populism.[12]

In Brazil the anti-Castro attitude taken for a time in 1960 by the Kubitschek administration was reversed early in 1961 by the new administration of President Janio Quadros. He stated publicly that Brazil would not support sanctions against the Castro regime, which the United States wished to impose. He likewise parted company with the United States on non-American questions, such as those relating to Red China and the Soviet satellite states of Eastern Europe. After less than a year in office Quadros resigned abruptly, but his successor, former Vice President João Goulart, continued his policy towards the Cuban question. Brazil's stand, coinciding with that taken by Mexico and Argentina, may have been decisive in preventing the imposition of sanctions on Cuba, for Brazil contains about one third of the total population of Latin America. Moreover, Goulart is the outstanding representative of populism in Brazil; and significantly, in the near-civil war that threatened to break out over the presidential succession when Quadros resigned, Goulart had the backing of a large part of the armed forces, despite the fact that these had hitherto traditionally supported the conservative classes.

These facts are doubly significant: first, because Brazil has hitherto been the staunchest ally of the United States among the Latin American states; and second, because Brazil has hitherto stood somewhat aside from the Spanish American states. It is still uncertain what the new direction given to Brazilian policy by Quadros and Goulart may portend for the future of populism and Pan Latin Americanism in Latin America at large, but apparently Brazil's great weight will be thrown behind the general Latin American trend of which we are speaking—the trend towards a strengthening of the solidarity of the Latin American group and a weakening of the group's ties with the United States.

The term "trend" is appropriate because the phenomenon in question is not new. Moreover, it is not exclusively the work of communists or left-wingers of the Castro type. The chief precedent of recent years was provided by the "Third Position" of Juan Perón's quasi fascist regime in Argentina in the 1940's and early '50's. As Perón explained it, the Third Position was neither a static nor an isolationist neutralism; rather, it was designed to align the Latin American nations in an independent group, uncommitted either to the East (the Soviet Union) or the West (the United States), and united in support of a dynamic policy aimed at promoting the distinctive interests of Latin America. The combined populist and anti-Yankee flavor of this policy was provided by the *descamisado* element in Perón's regime and this in turn had its precedents. An early presage came during the occupation of Cuba by the United States just after the Spanish American War, when it was found that "pro-United States sentiment was strongest among planters, merchants, and the upper classes generally," whereas Cuban nationalism and anti-United-States sentiment flourished mainly in the revolutionary party and the "propertyless" and largely illiterate working class. The suffrage was restricted accordingly.[13]

Another recent illustration of the trend in question is provided by the Bolivian national revolution since 1952. The nationalistic program of the party in control, the Movimiento Nacional Revolucionario (MNR), we are told, "virtually guaranteed its being skeptical, if not hostile, toward the United States." This was mainly because the program in question called for the expropriation of foreign-owned economic interests in which the United States was involved and the destruction of semi-feudal Bolivian latifundists who, according to the Marxist-Leninist doctrine prevalent among the MNR, were the allies of the North American "foreign imperialists."[14]

The United States decided in 1953 (contrary to the course it later took with regard to Castro's Cuba) to meet the Bolivian situation with a conciliatory policy which may be characterized as one of killing Marxism and Yankeephobia with kindness. Politically, this policy has so far been a success in the sense that Bolivia has not gone communist and has not broken with the United States—which, indeed, it could hardly do without immediately bankrupting itself. Economically, however, the experiment has hardly justified itself, for despite a substantial and steady flow of aid from the United States, Bolivia is nevertheless today on the verge of bankruptcy, so that even politically its prospects are not promising.

The net result is painful not only for Bolivia but for the United States as well. The ill-success of the experiment has fed skepticism in Latin America about the viability there of the whole system, both economic and political, represented by the United States. This skepticism in turn has rendered Latin Americans more responsive to one of the two main features of Fidel Castro's type of nationalism, namely, its exaltation of the authoritarian nation-state which sacrifices freedom to forced-draught economic development and social reform. There is obvious imitation here of the method employed with impressive success by the Soviet Union and Red China.

In the second feature of Castro's type of nationalism he has not only imitated the Soviet Union and Red China in this respect but has gone on to associate Cuba with them and the rest of the Communist bloc. The latter feature of Castro's nationalism has gained little acceptance in the rest of Latin America, where continental Americanism is still strong and where few share the naive belief, apparently entertained by Castro, that the lamb of Latin American nationalism can safely lie down with the Sino-Soviet lion. Purged of this offensive feature, Fidelismo could become a truly formidable force in Latin America at large, but the purge would wreck Castro's own regime by depriving it of Communist-bloc support, which has now become indispensable to it.

Castro's relative importance on the Latin American scale has been greatly exaggerated in the United States, on the apparent assumption that he is the key to the Latin American problem, that the Cuban tail wags the Latin American dog. Only some such miscalculation can explain the American government's support of the abortive invasion of Cuba in April, 1961. In fact Cuba is not a key but a sympton, and the general Latin American problem highlighted by it is one which by its very nature cannot be solved in any single country, since it is basically the problem of nationalism. But this is a variety of nationalism relatively new to most of Latin America. Its most distinctive ingredient is, not communism, but populism, which people in the United States ought to understand from their own nineteenth-century history. They must understand it if they are to deal with Latin America successfully on any other basis than coercion, for it has become a vital factor in all the "Big Three" countries— first in Mexico, then in Argentina, and more recently in Brazil—as well as in Cuba, Bolivia, and some of the other small countries that contain the remaining third of Latin America's population.

Why populism has become widespread in present-day Latin America is a question we cannot go into here. The point to be made is that its rise has reinforced nationalism in Latin America by giving this a broader popular base in each country. By the same token, it has also made Latin American nationalism more difficult for foreign countries such as the United States to cope with. How it will affect continental or Pan Latin American nationalism remains to be seen, though its initial effect, at least, seems likely to be adverse. In the next decade or two, even among the Spanish American nations Pan Latin Americanism will probably amount to little more than another name for international cooperation. As for that one third of Latin America called Brazil, its government's recent gestures towards closer ties with Spanish America, alluded to above, can hardly lead to anything more than a rather vague, and perhaps largely spiritual, solidarity.

7. Nationalism of the conventional type, modified only by the infusion of a populist strain, is still the dominant force in the key countries of Latin America. That area still has its full share of internecine rivalries between individual states and power blocs, not excluding those between large states and small. To mention only the three largest, one can hardly imagine either Mexico or Brazil or Argentina yielding any essential portion of their national individuality to a Latin American union, much less to an extra-American tie. The very limited concessions that seven of the Latin American states have made to their new Free Trade Association, under the Montevideo Treaty signed early in 1960, is about as far as any of them are likely to go towards continental nationalism in the guessable future. If the Central American states seem to be going further, let it

be remembered that this is in effect a return towards their original union of the 1820's and '30's. Indeed, the only relevant change of potentially great importance now afoot in Latin America is the rise of neutralism, and that is at bottom an assertion of the independence of each of them as regards the United States, and hence is only a fresh expression of conventional nationalism. Perón's dream of continentalizing his Third Position is still far from realization.

If any further change in the nationalist pattern in Latin America takes place in the decades just ahead, it is most likely to follow the Central American precedent of reconstituting a subregional union that existed in the past. Another such union might be that of the Bolivarian group in northern South America. Still another might be the Plata countries, with their viceregal tradition, of which the Argentine nationalist Ricardo Rojas wrote, nearly half a century ago, that they are joined by a "territorial consciousness founded in nature, which will tomorrow unite our nations of the littoral as in times past it united the interior provinces" of Argentina.

Whatever the future may hold, nationalism gives no sign of loosening the firm grip it has gained in Latin America—quite the contrary. Nor does the role of nationalism there show any sign of losing its great importance to the United States. In many ways it is a serious encumbrance to this country. The Latin Americans' economic nationalism is a bar to trade and investment; their cultural nationalism is a bar to communication; and their political nationalism has enormously complicated the problem posed for the United States by Fidel Castro's Cuba. Yet, on the other side of the ledger, their nationalism in all its aspects has been and still is, despite Cuba, in the cold war an asset to the United States and the free world at large, for it is the most effective of all barriers against penetration of the area by the Sino-Soviet bloc.

This concludes our rapid survey of three perspectives of nationalism in Latin America—global, local, and continental. Only too often it has had to be based on working hypotheses, for lack of a sounder historical infrastructure to build on. The relevant historical materials are still in large part unworked, but they are well worth thorough study, for the problem is one of great moment, whether viewed as past, present, or future. If Latin American nationalism is a challenge to policy makers in Washington, it is also a challenge to historians at large.

Notes

to the

Chapters

From Europe to Latin America

1. "Rehabilitación del nacionalismo?" in *Democracia, nacionalismo y militarismo* (Supplement to *Cuadernos*, Paris, Nov.-Dec., 1960), p. 15. This pamphlet reports views expressed at a symposium in Berlin, June, 1960; a similar yet different report is contained in *Preuves* (Paris), Oct., 1960, pp. 50-79.

2. *National Character* (rev. ed.; London: Methuen, 1948), p. 228. But note Johan Huizinga's view that nationalism is, not an instrument, but a "drive to dominate": *Men and Ideas* (New York: Meridian Books, 1959), p. 97.

3. *The Idea of Nationalism* (New York: Macmillan, 1960), pp. 10-13.

4. *Nationalism: A Religion* (New York: Macmillan, 1960), pp. 2-10.

5. Louis L. Snyder, *The Meaning of Nationalism* (New Brunswick, N. J.: Rutgers, 1954), pp. 74-111; see also Boyd C. Shafer, *Nationalism: Myth and Reality* (New York: Harcourt, Brace, 1955), *passim,* particularly useful for its extensive notes and bibliography. The related but separable and highly controversial question of national character is not discussed in the present volume; Snyder analyzes the problem well in chap. 8, but important additions have been made since he wrote.

6. William L. Langer, "The Next Assignment," *American*

Historical Review, LXIII (1958), 283-304; written without special reference to nationalism.

7. *Nationalism and Social Communication* (New York: Wiley, 1953).

8. This sketch is based mainly on the works of the two historians who have treated the subject most recently with a combination of broad perspective and concrete detail. The two men are Hans Kohn and Carlton Hayes.

9. Kohn, *Idea of Nationalism,* p. 168.

10. Ernest Barker, *Oliver Cromwell and the English People,* as quoted in Kohn, p. 168.

11. Kohn, *American Nationalism: An Interpretative Essay* (New York: Macmillan, 1957), pp. 21-29.

12. Arthur P. Whitaker, *The Western Hemisphere Idea: Its Rise and Decline* (Ithaca, N.Y.: Cornell, 1954), chaps. 1, 2.

13. Malbone W. Graham, *American Diplomacy in the International Community* (Baltimore: Johns Hopkins, 1948), chap. 1.

14. A convenient summary of Kohn's analysis, as developed at length in *The Idea of Nationalism* and other works, is in Snyder, *The Meaning of Nationalism,* pp. 118-20.

15. Arthur P. Whitaker, *Spain and Defense of the West* (New York: Harper, 1961), pp. 94-97.

16. Crane Brinton, *Ideas and Men: The Story of Western Thought* (New York: Prentice-Hall, 1950), pp. 416-20.

17. This is discussed by various authors in *Democracia, nacionalismo y militarismo.*

18. Albert Hourani, "El nacionalismo revolucionario," *ibid.,* p. 18.

19. Alfonso García Ruiz, *Ideario de Hidalgo* (Mexico City, Secretaría de Educación Pública, 1955), pp. 9-11.

20. Luis Monguió, "Nationalism and Social Discontent as Reflected in Spanish-American Literature," *The Annals,* American Academy of Political and Social Science, CCCXXXIV (1961), 65; see also an earlier article on the same subject: Gustavo Correa, "El nacionalismo en la literatura hispanoamericana," *Cuadernos americanos,* XCVIII (1958), 225-36.

21. "La manipulación del nacionalismo en Iberoamérica," *Examen* (Mexico City), May-June, 1959, pp. 18-20.

22. *Ibid.,* pp. 20-28.

The Case of Argentina

1. "La literatura y la formación de la conciencia nacional," *Política* (Caracas), Feb. 1960, pp. 75-77.

2. Narciso Binayán (ed.), *Ideario de Mayo* (Buenos Aires: Editorial Kapelusz, 1960), lxiv-lxvi; this volume contains some 215 documents of the period 1810-16.

3. Angel J. Battistessa, "Los modos espresivos de la literatura de Mayo," in *Algunos aspectos de la cultura literaria de Mayo* (La Plata: Universidad Nacional de la Plata, 1961), pp. 48-52.

4. Angel H. Azeves, "Mayo y el romanticismo literario," *ibid.*, p. 156.

5. José Luis Romero, *Mitre, un historiador frente al destino nacional* (privately printed, 1943).

6. As quoted by Domingo Sarmiento, who was in turn quoted by Carlos Pellegrini in his celebrated last speech to the Argentine Congress (June 11, 1906), San Martín said: "El ejército es un león que hay que tenerlo enjaulado para soltarlo el día de la batalla." Pellegrini, *Discursos y escritos: selección y estudio preliminar*, ed. José María Bustillo (Buenos Aires: Ediciones Estrada, 1959), p. 190.

7. *Ibid.*, p. cvii.

8. Although this title clearly connotes national pride, there is no good equivalent for it in English, since it involves an untranslatable play on words. *Blasón* means blazon, or heraldic shield, and *plata* means silver, so that a literal translation might be "Blazon (or Heraldic Shield) of Silver." But *blasón* also means honor, glory, and *plata* is also the name of a river intimately associated with the whole history of Argentina. To complicate matters still further, *argentina* means silvery, pertaining to silver, so that *plata* in the title could equally signify either silver, or the Plata River, or Argentina. Most probably the title was meant to signify "Glory of Argentina"; but the task of exegesis does not end here, for it should be pointed out that, to Rojas, Argentina rightfully meant the whole of the old Viceroyalty of La Plata, which included modern Uruguay, Paraguay, and southern Bolivia as well.

9. *La restauración nacionalista*, pp. 116-17.

10. *Ibid.*, pp. 154-60.

11. *Ensayo histórico sobre nuestra conciencia nacional en la gesta de la emancipación, 1810-1816* (2nd ed., *Obras de Ricardo Rojas*, t. III, Buenos Aires, 1922).

12. The English equivalent of *Indianismo* is, not Indianism, but nativism or Americanism. The word denotes a complex of several components, of which Indianism is only one. Even Rojas, who gave greater weight than most Argentines to the Indian component, also gave great weight to the others: the Spanish, the creole, and the "territorial" (a rather mystical concept of the spirit of the soil). This broad connotation of *Indianismo* has its roots in the colonial period, when Spain's American dominions were called *Las Indias* and *indianos* meant their inhabitants of Spanish origin, not the Indians, the term for whom was *indios*. This semantic problem

is important because of its bearing on the ideas of Rojas (and others) about Argentine nationalism and the differentiation of Argentina from other Latin American countries.

13. *Blasón de plata*, pp. 173-74; *El profeta de la pampa* (Buenos Aires: Losada, 1945), pp. 208-9. Rojas says Sarmiento's eyes were opened when he passed from theory to practice, for he then undertook a "tenacious campaign against cosmopolitanism" (*El profeta*, p. 631).

14. *La argentinidad*, pp. 7-8, 15; in the prologue (p. 7) he noted with satisfaction that *La restauración nacionalista* had won the applause of such *maestros de civilización* as Jean Juarès and Miguel de Unamuno in Europe and Roque Sáenz Peña, Rubén Darío, and José Enrique Rodó in America.

15. These paragraphs on Gálvez are based mainly on Otis H. Green, "Manuel Gálvez, 'Gabriel Quiroga,' and *La maestra normal*," *Hispanic Review*, XI (1943), 221-52, and to a lesser extent on Green's

other articles on Gálvez, *ibid.*, XI (1943), 314-27; XII (1944), 196-210.

16. Translated from the passage in *El solar de la raza* quoted *ibid.*, XII, 210 n, 57.

17. Clifton B. Kroeber, "Rosas and the Revision of Argentine History, 1880-1955," *Inter-American Review of Bibliography*, no. 9 (1960), 16.

18. José Luis Romero, "La crisis argentina: Realidad social y actividades políticas," *Política* (Caracas), no. 1 (1959), 86-96; Gino Germani, *Estratificación y movilidad social en Argentina, fuentes bibliográficas (1880-1958)* (Rio de Janeiro: Centro Latino-Americano de Investigaciones en Ciencias Sociales, 1959).

19. Speech to the United Nations General Assembly, Sept. 27, 1961, mimeographed text in Spanish.

20. Roberto Noble, *Argentina a World Power* (Buenos Aires: Arayú, 1961); this is an English translation of articles originally published in Noble's Buenos Aires newspaper, *Clarín*.

Continental Nationalism and the United States

1. Antonio Gómez Robledo, *Idea y experiencia de América* (Mexico City: Fondo de Cultura Económica, 1958), p. 73.

2. Although born (1768) and brought up in Peru, Egaña was the son of a Chilean, moved to Chile at the age of 21, and spent the rest of his life there.

3. Raúl Silva Castro, "Ideario Americanista de don Juan Egaña," *Revista de Historia de las Ideas*, no. 2 (1960), pp. 36-37.

4. *Ibid.*, 47-49.

5. "La variación hispano-americana," *Cuadernos* (Paris), Mar.-Apr., 1957, pp. 6-8.

6. *América en la historia*

(Mexico City: Fondo de Cultura Económica, 1957), *passim*.

7. "El nacionalismo cultural en la literatura hispanoamericana," *Cuadernos americanos*, XCVIII (1958), 225-36.

8. "El nacionalismo continental," *Examen* (Mexico City), Nov.-Dec., 1959, pp. 3-11.

9. "Problemas de la América Latina," *Cuadernos* (Paris), July-Aug., 1959, pp. 3-14.

10. A war between Chile and allied Peru and Bolivia.

11. "La manipulación del nacionalismo en Iberoamérica," *Examen* (Mexico City), May-June, 1959, pp. 18-29.

12. In this connection note should be made of a recent study which shows the preference of some Mexicans for Pan Latin Americanism over Pan Americanism: Jorge Castañeda, *Mexico and the United States* (New York: Manhattan, for El Colegio de México and the Carnegie Endowment for International Peace, 1958), chap. 7.

13. David F. Healy, *The Formation of America's Cuban Policy, 1898-1902* (unpublished Ph.D. thesis, University of Wisconsin, 1960), p. 182.

14. Robert J. Alexander, *The Bolivian National Revolution* (New Brunswick, N.J.: Rutgers, 1958), p. 256.

List of
Additional
Readings

The books and articles listed below supplement the citations in the text and footnotes, which are not repeated here.

ALBA, Víctor, "Mitología del movimiento obrero: el nacionalismo proletario," *Cuadernos Americanos*, XIII, no. 5 (1954), 43-57.

ALBERINI, Coriolano, "La enseñanza de la historia en las universidades alemanas," *Nosotros*, VI, no. 36 (1912), 56-64.

ARDAO, Arturo. *La filosofía en el Uruguay en el siglo XX.* Mexico City, 1956.

ATUÑA, José G. "Vers l'expression américaine: le sens d'histoire et le nationalisme dans l'oeuvre de Ricardo Rojas," *Revue de l'Amérique Latine* (1928), 481-90.

AYALA, Francisco, "El nacionalismo sano y el otro," *Sur*, no. 242 (1956), 5-10.

BASADRE, Jorge, "Why Nationalism?" *Americas*, I, no. 7 (1949), 12-14.

BELAUNDE, Víctor Andrés. *Bolívar and the Political Thought of the Spanish American Revolution.* Baltimore, 1938.

CARRILLO FLORES, Antonio, "El nacionalismo de los paises latinoamericanos en la postguerra," *Jornadas*, no. 28 (1945).

CLINE, Howard F. "Mexico: A Matured Latin-American Revolution," *The Annals*, American Academy of Political and Social Science, March, 1961, pp. 84-94.

DUŸKER, H. C. J., and N. H. Frÿda, *National Character and National Stereotypes: A Trend Report Prepared for the International Union of Scientific Psychology.* Amsterdam: North Holland Publishing Co., 1960.

EDWARDS BELLO, Joaquín. *Nacionalismo continental.* Santiago, 1935.

EZCURRA MEDRANO, Alberto. *Catolicismo y nacionalismo.* Buenos Aires: Adsum, 1939.

FILLOL, Tomás Roberto. *Social Factors in Economic Development.* Cambridge, Mass.: M.I.T. Press, 1961.

FITZGIBBON, Russell H. *Uruguay, Portrait of a Democracy.* New Brunswick, N. J., 1954.

FRONDIZI, Arturo. *Petróleo y política: contribución al estudio de la historia económica argentina y de las relaciones entre el imperialismo y la vida política nacional.* Buenos Aires, 1954.

GAMIO, Manuel. *Forjando patria (pro nacionalismo).* Mexico City, 1916.

GIUSTI, Roberto F. "La restauración nacionalista," *Nosotros,* IV, no. 26 (1910), 139-54.

GLAUERT, Earl T. "The Cultural Nationalism of Ricardo Rojas." Ph.D. dissertation, University of Pennsylvania, 1962.

GONZÁLEZ, Joaquín V. *La tradición nacional.* 2 vols. Buenos Aires, 1912.

HANSON, Simon G. *Utopia in Uruguay.* New York, 1938.

HARRISON, John P. "The Confrontation with the Political University," *The Annals,* American Academy of Political and Social Science, March, 1961, pp. 74-83.

INGENIEROS, José. *Por la unión latino americana.* Buenos Aires, 1922.

JOHNSON, John J. *Political Change in Latin America: The Emergence of the Middle Sectors.* Stanford, Calif.: Stanford University Press, 1948.

JUSTO, Juan Bautista. *Discursos y escritos políticos.* Buenos Aires, 1933.

KENNEDY, John J. *Catholicism, Nationalism and Democracy in Argentina.* Notre Dame, Ind.: University of Notre Dame Press, 1958.

KOHN, Hans. *The Age of Nationalism: The First Era of Global History.* New York: Harper, 1962.

LA FERRERE, Roberto de. *El nacionalismo de Rosas.* Buenos Aires: Haz, 1953.

LIPPMANN, Walter. "Vested Rights and Nationalism in Latin America," *Foreign Affairs,* April, 1927, 353-63.

D 410 F71

MENDIETA Y NUÑEZ, Lucio. "La clase media en México," *Revista Mexicana de Sociología*, XVII, no. 2-3 (1955), 517-31.

MONTEMAYOR, Mariano. "Los corrientes políticos en Hispano-américa," *Dinámica Social*, II, no. 13-14 (1951), 18-19.

MONTENEGRO, Carlos. *Nacionalismo y coloniaje*. 2nd ed., La Paz, 1943.

MOSK, Sanford A. "El nacionalismo económico en la América Latina," *Revista de Economía Continental*, I, no. 4 (1946), 401-11.

OTERO, Gustavo Adolfo. *Sociología del nacionalismo en Hispano-América*. Quito, 1947.

PLATT, Washington. *National Character in Action: Intelligence Factors in Foreign Relations*. New Brunswick, N. J.: Rutgers University Press, 1961.

POTTER, David M. *People of Plenty: Economic Abundance and the American Character*. Chicago: University of Chicago Press, 1954.

ROMERO, José Luis. *Las ideas políticas en Argentina*. Mexico City: Fondo de Cultura Económica, 1946.

SILVERT, K. H. "Nationalism in Latin America," *The Annals*, American Academy of Political and Social Science, March, 1961, pp. 10-19.

TANNENBAUM, Frank. "Agrarismo, Indianismo, y Nacionalismo," *Hispanic American Historical Review*, XXIII (1943), 394-423.

TRONCOSO, Oscar A. *Los nacionalistas argentinos*. Buenos Aires: Ed. Saga, 1957.

VARELA, A. H. *El nacionalismo y los obreros socialistas*. 2nd ed. Buenos Aires: Padilla y Contreras, 1944.

VASCONCELOS, José. *Hispanoamérica frente a los nacionalismos agresivos de Europa y Norteamérica*. Buenos Aires, 1934.

WAISS, Oscar. *Nacionalismo y socialismo en América Latina*. Santiago, 1954.

Index

ABC bloc: formation, 22
Africa: nationalism in, 14, 16, 18, 24, 56, 64-65
Alba, Víctor: cited, 21, 23-24, 68, 69
Alberdi, Juan Bautista: and liberal nationalism, 34, 46
Anticlericalism in Argentina, 41
Aprista party: mentioned, 62
Argentina: nationalism in, 18, 19, 21, 22, 23, 25-54; ties with Europe, 25-26, 30-31; adoption of name, 27; "canonical nationalism," 28-38, 41; role of the military, 35-37, 48-49; economic nationalism, 35, 37-38, 40-41, 44, 47-53; populism, 74. *See also* Perón, Juan; Perón regime
"Argentina a World Power": described, 52
Argentinidad La: described, 39, 43-44
Ariel: published, 22
Asia: nationalism in, 12, 14, 16, 18, 24

BARKER, Ernest: cited, 3
Barreda Laos, Felipe: cited, 67-68
Batlle y Ordóñez, José: as reformer and nationalist, 22
Belgrano, Manuel: biography of, 35-37
Blasón de plata: described, 39, 42
Bolívar, Simón: and nationalism, 19, 56, 63, 65
Bolivia: mentioned, 64; nationalism in, 73, 74
Braganza: house of, 18-19
Brazil: nationalism in, 18, 22, 70, 71-72, 74; mentioned, 25, 59, 64
Buenos Aires: ties with Europe, 25-26; British attack on (1806-7), 27

CASTRO, Fidel: activities in Latin America, 60; relation to communism and populism, 69-74
Central America: cooperation in, 75-76
Chile: nationalism in, 22, 56-58

87

Hayes, Carlton: cited, 4, 12
Hidalgo, Bartolomé: Uruguayan writer, 32
Hidalgo y Costilla, Miguel: as nationalist, 19
Hispano-América en guerra?: described, 67-68

IBARGUREN, Carlos: and Rosas cult, 44-45
Independence, Latin American: centennial celebrations, 22
Indianismo: defined, 42
Indigenous American cultures: relation to nationalism, 23
International Monetary Fund: mentioned, 51
Investments, foreign: Latin American attitudes towards, 21, 35, 47, 76; effects, 58
Irigoyen, Hipólito: as nationalist, 37, 48, 50; ousted, 46, 48
Italy: and Argentina, 47, 49

JAMAICA Letter: mentioned, 56
Jovellanos, Gaspar Melchor de: as Spanish writer, 31
Justo, Juan Bautista: cited, 21, 37

KOHN, Hans: cited, 4, 12

LABOR, Latin American organized. *See* names of international organizations
Latin America: in world affairs, 59-60
Latin American Confederation of Labor: established, 60
Latin American Free Trade Association: mentioned, 75
Liberalism: relation to nationalism, 13-14, 20, 33-35, 40, 42-43
Lima conferences, 1847 and 1865: mentioned, 58
Lira argentina, La: published, 28, 29
López y Planes, Vicente: as nationalist writer, 27
Lugones, Leopoldo: as exponent of nationalism, 44
Lüthy, Herbert: cited, 3

MAÑACH, Jorge: cited, 61
Mann, Horace: and Argentina, 35
Marseillaise: echoed in Argentina, 31
Martín Fierro: relation to nationalism, 44
Martínez Estrada, Ezequiel: as critic of Argentine nationalism, 28, 30
Mexico: nationalism in, 18-19, 22-23, 48, 70-71, 74; mentioned, 25
Middle class, Latin American: and nationalism, 22, 24; in Argentina, 47
Middle East: nationalism in, 16
Military, role of: in Brazil, 71; in Argentina, 35-37, 48-49
Mitre, Bartolomé: as Argentine nationalist, 33-37
Montevideo Treaty, 1960: mentioned, 75
Movimiento Nacional Revolucionario: mentioned, 72

NAPOLEON, 1, 11
Nationalism: meaning, 2-6; functional interpretation, 7-11, 31-32; stages of development, 11-14; rehabilita-

Social change: relation to nationalism, 26, 47-51
Socialist party, Argentine: and economic nationalism, 21
Soviet Union: mentioned, 70, 73
Spain: nationalism in, 12-13, 14, 18; revolt in America against, 27, 28, 36; literary influence in Argentina, 31, 34, 44

THIRD Position: term explained, 72; mentioned, 76
Traditionalism: as variant of nationalism, 45

UNITED Nations: Latin Americans in, 60
United States: nationalism in, 2, 3, 7, 9-11, 19; Latin American views of, 44, 46, 48, 59, 63, 66-68, 69-73; and Argentina, 51
Uruguay: nationalism in, 22; mentioned, 32, 67

VARELA, Juan Cruz: as nationalist writer, 28
Vendepatrias: charges against, 22, 48, 51
Venezuela: nationalism in, 22
Viceroyalty of Buenos Aires: tradition of, 31, 53

WAR of the Pacific: mentioned, 63
Western Hemisphere idea: relation to nationalism, 10, 65, 68
World Confederation of Free Trade Unions: mentioned, 60
World War I: mentioned, 59
World War II: mentioned, 59, 69

YACIMIENTOS Petrolíferos Fiscales: established, 38, 50

ZEA, Leopoldo: cited, 61, 65